RUGBY
LEAGUE

BRING YOUR A GAME

Also by Anthony Sharwood

From Snow to Ash

The Brumby Wars

Kosciuszko

THE ENCYCLOPAEDIA

BRING YOUR A GAME

OF AUSTRALIAN SPORTS CLICHES

ANTHONY SHARWOOD

Illustrated by Louisa Maggio

hachette AUSTRALIA

hachette
AUSTRALIA

Published in Australia and New Zealand in 2024
by Hachette Australia
(an imprint of Hachette Australia Pty Limited)
Gadigal Country, Level 17, 207 Kent Street, Sydney, NSW 2000
www.hachette.com.au

Hachette Australia acknowledges and pays our respects to the past, present and future Traditional Owners and Custodians of Country throughout Australia and recognises the continuation of cultural, spiritual and educational practices of Aboriginal and Torres Strait Islander peoples. Our head office is located on the lands of the Gadigal people of the Eora Nation.

NATIONAL LIBRARY OF AUSTRALIA

A catalogue record for this book is available from the National Library of Australia

ISBN: 978 0 7336 5259 2 (hardback)

Cover design by Louisa Maggio
Internal illustrations by Louisa Maggio
Typeset in Simoncini Garamond by Kirby Jones
Printed and bound in Australia by McPherson's Printing Group

FSC www.fsc.org MIX Paper | Supporting responsible forestry FSC® C001695

The paper this book is printed on is certified against the Forest Stewardship Council® Standards. McPherson's Printing Group holds FSC® chain of custody certification SA-COC-005379. FSC® promotes environmentally responsible, socially beneficial and economically viable management of the world's forests.

BRING YOUR A GAME

INTRODUCTION

When a cliche paints a thousand words

As cliches go, this one took the cake and ate it too.

Immediately after the third men's cricket Test between Australia and Pakistan in January 2024, Australian sports website foxsports.com.au published their regular post-series player ratings. Australian wicketkeeper Alex Carey scored seven out of ten overall after a reasonable series with the bat, but it was his glovework behind the stumps that really impressed.

'Carey didn't put a foot wrong with the gloves against Pakistan,' *Fox Sports* wrote.

Um ... what??? Carey didn't put a *foot* wrong with the gloves???

Did the journalist realise what he had written? Did he understand that he had used a foot cliche for a hand activity? Did he not consider employing another turn of phrase? If he really wanted to use a cliche, surely he could have used a neutral one and written something like Carey 'didn't miss a trick' with the gloves? He might even have gone for a body-appropriate cliche and said Carey was 'a deft touch' or 'a sure hand'.

But no, the journalist wrote that Carey 'didn't put a foot wrong', which you have to say is a classic case of foot in mouth or, in this case, foot in glove.

How did it happen?

Possibly the journalist was inexperienced, or in a hurry, or both, and simply didn't notice. Maybe there was no subeditor 'on hand' to put their 'foot down', and indeed that's often the case these days, which is why you'll often read that a player was 'wrapped' instead of 'rapt', which is a shortened form of 'enraptured', as in extremely happy. But it's also possible that an experienced subeditor read the copy and didn't notice. That wouldn't be surprising because sports cliches are so ubiquitous in Australian sporting language, we're barely aware we're using them.

This is not always a bad thing.

A cliche is 'a phrase or opinion that is overused and betrays a lack of original thought', states the first entry when you type the phrase 'definition of cliche' into Google. 'A phrase, remark, or opinion that has very often been said or expressed before and is therefore not original and not interesting' says the second entry. You get the idea.

The very definition of the word cliche has a negative connotation according to the gatekeepers of the English language. It's like, 'Come on, people, can't you do better? Tens of thousands of words in the English language, infinite combinations of those words, and you're still arranging the same few words in dog-eared old phrases and idioms again and again?'

To a degree, the professional wordsmiths have a point. Sports cliches can indeed be turgid. Strung together one after the other, it can feel like the commentary or match report or whatever you're listening to or reading was composed by artificial intelligence. At the risk of stating the bleeding obvious, using cliches like they're going out of style should be avoided like the plague. The back-to-back cliches in the previous sentence are the proof in the pudding!

But sports cliches also serve an important function. Used sparingly, sports cliches are familiar little nuggets which tell the reader or viewer, or your best mate, that you're on the same page. They're like passwords that gain you entry to a club, and acceptance within that club.

When sports fans banter among ourselves while watching sport or when dissecting the weekend's results, cliches are little signs that say we speak a common tongue. We talk about a player bringing their A-game and nobody thinks they've spent the last two hours playing Scrabble. We talk about a glut of possession and nobody thinks we're talking about Gina Rinehart's assets or Clive Palmer's kitchen pantry. We talk about playing the whistle and nobody thinks you've taken up the kazoo.

We speak of premiership windows without thinking of glass, of premiership droughts without thinking of grass, of schooling an opponent without imagining them in class.

We talk of a team being a well-oiled machine or a player being an excitement machine, and nobody thinks we're fixated upon adult toys. We know that the coaching merry-go-round is not a carnival ride, that a ball magnet is not the latest James Bond gadget, and that even uphill battles are fought on level playing fields.

We talk of good teams on paper, only to discover that they have paper-thin defence, but in neither case do we imagine it involves origami.

When the TV cameras take us to the 'inner sanctum', we know they mean the dressing rooms. When AFL teams speak of the Holy Grail, we know they're not searching for the elusive prize in the Monty Python movie.

When a team is at sixes and sevens, we know it has nothing to do with numbers. When a player vows to give 110 per cent, we know that it's mathematically impossible but we understand that they'll give their all. When a coach has a selection headache, we know they're not choosing between a migraine and a hangover. And speaking of hangovers, when a team has a premiership hangover, we know that even the most intense alcohol-fuelled celebrations don't last into the next season even if premiership hangovers (in the sense of a premiership team playing poorly the next season) often do.

Sports cliches are like a ticket to the game. They put us in a moulded plastic seat with a beer and hot chips on our lap. They are a sports fan's verbal comfort food. That right there was a cliche to describe an entire subgenre of cliches – and that's precisely the point. The instant familiarity of cliches is what makes them valuable, important, even necessary. A cliched phrase is like an electric pulse in the brain, connecting familiarity to understanding, and understanding to belonging.

And sport, at its heart, is about belonging.

You belong to a team. You belong to a group of fans who support the team. You belong to the wider sporting community as a player, former player, volunteer, official, fan, tragic, weekend warrior or all of the above. In all aspects of life, from the workplace to the family and everywhere in between, we reinforce our belonging through our vocabulary, and cliches are a huge part of how we do that in sport.

This book started as a thought bubble.

As a sports fan and former sports writer for magazines, newspapers, websites and television, I've used as many sports cliches as anyone in my time, sometimes deliberately, sometimes unwittingly. Occasionally, I've pondered how amusing some cliches are in literal terms, and how funny they'd look if you could bring them to life.

And then the idea began to coalesce like rugby players forming a scrum: what if we brought some key Australian sporting cliches to life? In these pages, Louisa Maggio's brilliant illustrations do exactly that.

We've all heard talk of players who are 'under an injury cloud', as though they are cowered under a large grey cumulonimbus. Now we can all picture that scene for ourselves.

We've all heard of players who seize key moments by 'taking the game by the scruff of the neck'. Okay, let's see that mother cat with its kitten.

We speak of victory snatched from the jaws of defeat. So let's see those fearsome teeth up close.

But this book also goes beyond the world of cliches.

As I started writing about sports cliches, I realised that Australian sporting language is an entire dialect which no one has written about in its own right. There are books of Australian slang phrases and books of great Australian sporting tales, yet where is the book that specifically celebrates the language of Australian sport? It's here in your hands, that's where.

This book is an exploration and a celebration of our incredibly rich sporting lexicon. The key word there is 'celebrated' because this is not a bland dictionary of Australian sporting jargon, or a listicle in book form (which, when you think about it, is exactly what a dictionary is). Nor does this book pretend to provide an exhaustive list of every single Australian sporting cliche, term, phrase, idiom and expression, because you'd have to visit every stadium, living room, dressing room and pub in Australia to capture that.

This book is a tribute to the wonderful sporting jargon used by Australians, most of which is uniquely ours, and is therefore unintelligible to citizens of just about every other nation. If one of your favourites didn't make the cut, get in touch.

Above all, this book is an unapologetic up-yours to the compilers of dictionaries or anyone else who reckons cliches betray a lack of original thought. The richness and humour in Australian sports cliches, and in our broader sporting vocabulary, is the complete opposite of unoriginality.

So let's raise a glass half full to Aussie sports lingo and take this one cliche at a time.

WORLD OF PAIN

Reserved for a player who has been severely injured in a jarring tackle, a brutal blow in a combat sport, or who has suffered some other grave misfortune on the sporting field, we've all heard a commentator's anguished tones as they go, 'Oh, they are living in a world of pain right now.' Spare a thought for poor old Globey here. And note that it includes Cuba. Why does that matter? Because the socialist Caribbean nation of just 11 million citizens sits a very close second on the all-time Olympic boxing medal tally with forty-two gold medals to the USA's fifty, and eighty boxing medals overall to the USA's 118. The success is due to the communist regime introducing boxing programs after the Cuban revolution in 1959. As for poor old Australia, we've won a silver and six bronze but never Olympic boxing gold. You have to say it: the Australian boxing community will be living in a world of pain until we claim that elusive gold.

Great Aussie sporting terms: *Versing*

This one is controversial, but this book is testament to the fact that language evolves, and did not that great sage Whitney Houston tell us that the children are the future? We therefore present to you the word 'versing', a derivative of the term 'versus', used in sentences like 'The Bulldogs are versing the Tigers this week.'

It makes sense, people. You know it does. Before the current generation of kids started using this word, you had to construct a clunky sentence along the lines of 'The Bulldogs are playing the Tigers this week' or 'The Bulldogs are up against the Tigers this week' when the match up ahead was Bulldogs versus Tigers. To say 'The Bulldogs are versing the Tigers' is an elegant solution. Like every great Australian backyard DIY job, it takes the spare parts lying around and fashions them into something useful. Better than useful, in fact. Indispensable! Let the diehards fight this one – I used to be one of them, chapter and 'verse' – but the diehards will lose, and deservedly so.

Every kid in Australia uses the word versing nowadays. They don't even know it's technically not a word. The future is here and there is no going in 'reverse'.

Great Aussie sporting terms: *Footy*

'Footy' might be the greatest, most unique and most useful Australian sporting word of them all. The British have an archaic word for soccer – footer – which no one really uses anymore, and which is probably the linguistic foundation of the word 'footy'. But footy is our word and it's ubiquitous when talking about Aussie rules football and rugby league, and used frequently but not always with rugby union. It is even occasionally used for the game the rest of the world calls football (as in soccer).

Where would we be without the word footy? You follow the footy. You go to the footy. You play footy. You kick the footy. There is footy season, footy tipping and footy fever at finals time. When Channel 9 had TV shows about footy in both the NRL and AFL, they obviously called both of them *The Footy Show*. The word footy is indispensable. *The Footy Shows* (RIP), not so much.

Many people still get the lingo around the various footy codes wrong, despite our increasing sporting bilingualism. The state of Victoria will probably slide into the Southern Ocean before the majority of its citizens call rugby league 'rugby league' rather than 'rugby'.

'Rugby' is the most common global name for the sport officially called rugby union, and used to distinguish it from rugby league. If we're going with one word, it's 'rugby' for rugby union and 'league' for rugby league, but never, *ever* rugby for rugby league. That'd be like calling a sausage roll a sausage.

As for Australian rules football, aka Aussie rules football, Aussie rules, Australian football or even just football, it's undergoing something of a name crisis. To many people, the name of the national professional competition has become synonymous with the sport itself. This is especially true outside the traditional football states, where people often call the game 'AFL'.

My youngest kid played junior footy in Sydney, as in junior Aussie rules, and all the kids called it 'AFL'. You couldn't get them to call it 'footy' because 'footy' in Sydney generally means rugby league. You couldn't explain that playing AFL literally means playing senior professional footy, and you couldn't get them to call it Australian rules football or Aussie rules because the kids literally had no idea about the sport's official name. AFL it was.

One defiant man rails daily against the madness of those who refer to the sport by the name of its pre-eminent national competition and governing body. He prefers not to disclose his real name, which is refreshing in an age when everyone online is seeking attention, but he goes by @AFLisnotasport on Twitter (or X or whatever they call it now), and tirelessly calls out anyone who calls the sport AFL, including the very junior club for which my son played, whose Twitter profile says: 'We welcome boys and girls who want to have fun, meet friends, and play AFL!'

They should have just said play footy. Why waste such an excellent word?

Great Aussie sporting terms: *Average*

Being average in Australian sport doesn't literally mean you're average, as in you possess an ability level which places you roughly in the middle of the pack. It means you're bloody hopeless and lucky to get a game in the reserves, or the 'twos' as they say in Aussie rules footy.

Speaking of 'twos', there was a Test cricketer in the late 1990s called Roger Twose, pronounced exactly thus, as in 'he scored a lot of ones and twos'. A left-handed batter, Twose emigrated from England to New Zealand to chase his dream of playing Test cricket. This he achieved, although with a meagre average of

A BLEND OF YOUTH AND EXPERIENCE

As mentioned in 'premiership window' (page 88), all good teams need a blend of youth and experience, though it's probably best if you don't actually throw them in an actual kitchen blender!

25 after sixteen Tests, you'd have to say he was, in the Australian sense, very average.

Great Aussie sporting terms: *Speccy*

There are many ways to spell this one. The main three options seem to be specky, speckie and speccy but we'll go with the latter. However you spell it, speccies are spectacular, unsurprising given they seem to have originated from that word.

A speccy is a mark in Aussie rules footy where a player flies high above the pack. It's often also called a 'screamer' or a 'hanger' because a player's 'hang time' is exaggerated by their perching on the shoulders or back of an unfortunate opponent.

Speccies are one of the main reasons we watch the game. They're also why we have the phrase and famous song 'Up There Cazaly', an anthemic tribute to St Kilda and South Melbourne legend Roy Cazaly, who was renowned for soaring high and dragging the ball down from the clouds. Interestingly, Cazaly played ninety-nine games for each club but never won a premiership, but it's a measure of how much we love the speccy that no one would ever call Cazaly's career incomplete.

Spectacular Aussie sporting names: *Steele Sidebottom*

Along with Scott Pendlebury, Steele Sidebottom is the only Collingwood player who featured in both the 2010 and 2023 AFL premierships. Oh, but you don't care about his longevity. You want to know about that name.

Official AFL publication *The AFL Record* ran a great story on the history of the Sidebottom clan involving convict transport from England and all kinds of colonial skulduggery in Van Diemen's Land and early Melbourne. Sadly, there was no mention of the name's etymological origin, although the article did mention that back in the day, a family member insisted that it be pronounced 'Siddy-b'tarm'. Steele Sidebottom has no such pretensions and proudly owns his unusual name, which of course was shared by the late Garry Sidebottom, a VFL and WAFL star of the seventies and eighties who was probably no relation and whose most famous moment was missing the team bus to the 1981 preliminary final against Collingwood, which his team, Geelong, lost by seven points.

Oh, and speaking of people in Australian sport with the first name Steele, rugby league player Steele Retchless racked up thirty-three games in the 1990s in what was then called the ARL, while Steele Tallon is the head of media and communications for the Brisbane Broncos, and before that had the same gig with the Brisbane Lions. If Steele Tallon's name sounds like the claws on some sort of lethal robot eagle, rest assured that he is actually a delightful fellow.

Great Aussie sporting terms: *Mullygrubber*

Of all the words Australia has given cricket, 'mullygrubber' is probably the greatest. It is a ball that skids along the ground, usually by accident due to the quirks and eccentricities of a cricket pitch. We also have a word for its opposite. A ball which doesn't bounce and travels through at a dangerous height is a 'beamer', similar to the American term 'beanball' for a ball pitched deliberately at an opponent's head. Beamers (usually) aren't deliberate, but a bowler can still be banned from bowling if they send down more than one. A bowler who bowls too many beamers and mullygrubbers? They're on display every weekend in social cricket around the country, or in English county cricket, and they are known as 'pie chuckers'.

Great Aussie sporting terms: *Barrack*

Barrack is such a common word in the so-called AFL states that most locals have no idea it's a uniquely Australian term. But it is. No other country uses it the way we do, and indeed only about half the country regularly uses it in the context of cheering for a team or player. The word is not unknown in New South Wales and Queensland, but it's much less common. You'd certainly rarely ask a person in New South Wales or Queensland which NRL team they barrack for. You'd more likely ask who they 'support' or 'go for'. And when a person from those two states yells from the sideline, most would tell you that they're cheering.

Further afield, in England, 'barrack' has a negative connotation of criticising or abusing players. Only in Australia is it a positive, supportive act.

So how exactly do Australians barrack? In most sports we don't sing like European football fans, but when you buy a ticket to a sporting arena, you buy the right to scream till your throat is dry – as long as you don't vilify anyone along racial or other lines. In short, we shout. A lot.

As the third stanza of the Collingwood club song goes:

See the barrackers a shouting,

As all barrackers should.

The fourth and final stanza of that song also bears a quick mention:

Oh, the premiership's a cakewalk,

For the good old Collingwood

Side note: there are three ways of looking at the claim that premierships are a 'cakewalk' for Collingwood, the Australian sporting team with the most members (106,000 in 2024) and without doubt the most haters, even though there's no official stat for that.

First, it's true: as of its 2023 premiership, Collingwood has won the equal-most VFL/AFL premierships (sixteen) alongside Essendon and Carlton since 1897.

Second, it's false: Collingwood has failed to win twenty-nine grand finals, including twenty-seven losses and two draws. No other club has lost half that many.

Third, it's hilarious. Well, it is! The word 'cakewalk' is an amusing choice in football, or any context. The word has its origins in African American culture among the enslaved before the Civil War, when it was the name of a type of dance. But the term has morphed into everyday use among English speakers of all cultures, coming to mean something easily attained or not difficult.

Personally, I've always thought Collingwood should take the phrase seriously. Remember when teams used to jog victory laps after winning a grand final? Now those laps are walked, taking a good half-hour or longer, as the victorious players pose for selfies with friends, family and fans. If the premiership really is a cakewalk for Collingwood, turn it into one! Give Nick Daicos, Scott Pendlebury and friends a slice of cake on paper plates to

KEEN STUDENT OF THE GAME

A keen student of the game is a player with a deep understanding of their chosen sport's history, culture and the technicalities of the sport. The way you attain that knowledge is of course to live, breathe and play the game over many years. Or apparently you can go to footy school to learn it!

eat as they circle The 'G. As a symbol of their supremacy, let them eat cake – and walk. You know it makes sense.

Great Aussie sporting terms: *Stoked*

When three-time world surfing champion Mick Fanning had a run-in with a shark, his compatriot and mate Julian Wilson furiously paddled toward him to lend assistance before Fanning was scooped up by an official on a jet ski.

The duo were contesting the final of the 2015 J-Bay Open at Jeffreys Bay, South Africa, and the event was immediately called off, with the final declared a draw.

Even though the event ended prematurely, the media wheels kept turning as a still-wet and visibly shaken Fanning immediately did an interview to camera. The interview should probably have been cancelled too, but boy, was it compelling viewing. Fanning was talking way too fast and clearly still in shock, so he was not making a whole lot of sense. You could see him trying to piece the events together in his mind even as he described them to the interviewer. The interview lasted a touch over two minutes.

And at the end, Fanning took a deep breath, exhaled like he'd never exhaled before and said, 'To walk away from that, I'm just so stoked. Oh, man.'

Of course he said he was stoked. What else would he say?

'Stoked' is the most Aussie surfing word of them all, and perhaps the most Aussie word full stop. Californian surfers reckon they invented the word 'stoked' and maybe that's true, but the British invented meat pies and Australians made them our own. Same deal with 'stoked'. Seems like these days, surfies can barely string a sentence together without using the word, and it has migrated into the broader culture too, and especially youth culture.

'Stoked' is by no means the Australian surf scene's only contribution to our lingo. With 35,877 kilometres of coastline (or 38,907 kilometres if you include Tasmania) surf culture, and beach culture more generally, is central to the Australian identity, so it's no surprise a vast swathe of our vocabulary relates to it, some of which has migrated overseas, some of which hasn't. Only in Australia do we call swimwear 'swimmers', 'cossies' or 'boardies' and wetsuits 'wetties'. One of the greatest Aussie surf words is 'esky lid', meaning a bodyboard. That's a case of double slang, because only Australians call portable coolers 'eskies'. Another great

Aussie surf word is 'grommets' or 'groms' for young surfers or bodyboarders. That one has definitely become part of the global surf lingo.

We even have two great terms for sharks: there's 'men in grey suits' and then there's 'Noahs', as in Noah's arks, a classic piece of Aussie rhyming slang.

The rescue jet ski would have looked as big as an ark to Mick Fanning at J-Bay that day in 2015, that's for sure.

Great Aussie sporting terms: *Got 'im, yes!*

Bill Lawry's old-school cricket commentary had plenty of stock phrases. When a Victorian player in the Australian cricket team did something good, the proud Victorian pigeon fancier would always remind viewers, 'And he's a Victorian!' In One Day cricket matches in the summer holidays, Lawry used to say, 'It's a happy crowd, it's a holiday crowd', which was always a bit weird, but that was our Bill.

But if you had to reduce Lawry's ultra-excitable on-mic persona to one phrase, it'd undoubtedly be 'Got 'im, yes!' That's what he would say when there was a catch in the infield.

'Got 'im, yes!'

Or a catch in the outfield.

'Got 'im, yes!'

Or any form of dismissal.

'Got 'im, yes!'

The phrase is now part of everyday Australian speech. Successfully swat a mosquito on the back porch? 'Got 'im, yes!' Throw a scrunched-up sandwich bag in the bin from seven paces away as you walk down the street? 'Got 'im, yes!' You get the idea.

Great Aussie sporting terms: *Roughie*

There are so many great Australian horse racing words. Nowhere else on Earth is the sport as mainstream, even in this age when the Melbourne Cup is experiencing a bit of a dip in popularity due to criticism from once-a-year animal welfare activists.

Many of the best words revolve around the act of betting. Fluctuations in the betting market are ubiquitously called 'flucs', runners whose odds shorten are called 'firmers', while runners whose odds lengthen due to a lack of betting interest are called 'drifters'. When big money comes for a horse, it's called a 'plunge' or a 'plonk'. If a plunge comes off, you'll be encouraged to 'get in the jolly old queue'. Race callers use this one all the time and it's surely the only instance in the full breadth of human experience when queueing can be said to be a jolly experience.

Perhaps the greatest Australian word with regard to betting or odds is 'roughie'. Most countries use the word 'longshot' but we use 'roughie' or sometimes 'bolter' for a horse that is considered unlikely to win and is therefore at long odds. A horse that bolts is one that takes off in an uncontrollable manner, hence the term bolter, as such a horse would be unlikely to win after expending too much energy early. As for roughie, the term describes itself. The horse's chances are rough. Perhaps it even physically looks rougher than the rest of the field. There was a champion in the early to mid-1990s called Rough Habit, which won twenty-seven races. They used to call him 'Old Roughie', which was our laconic way of saying that he was absolutely not that in terms of ability.

Australia is also way ahead of the world in the way it represents odds. We used to use the old fractional odds which are still commonplace in countries like the UK. For example, in England, they'd say that the favourite is 6/4, an antiquated expression of the win/loss probability. We would simply say the horse's odds are $2.50. Australia used the UK system till about the 1990s, when we switched to expressing odds in terms of the return for a $1 investment. It's such a simple and elegant idea. Why doesn't everyone do it?

Great Aussie sporting quirks: *Our Great Sporting Divide*

I grew up in a bilingual household. My family spoke the language of both AFL and NRL – or at least VFL and NSWRL, as they were called

SNATCH VICTORY FROM THE JAWS OF DEFEAT

As detailed in our discussion of the word 'stoked', (page 30), Mick Fanning literally did this – if you take victory as surviving and defeat as the unthinkable opposite. The cliche can also work in reverse, with commentators sometimes speaking of teams or players who snatch defeat from the jaws of victory. There was no better exponent of this dark art than Greg Norman (see page 102).

back in the dark mists of the 1980s. This was not the experience of most Australians.

Winter team sports in Australia were two different universes and in many ways, they still are. The country still has a Great Sporting Divide, with the majority of people in Queensland and New South Wales favouring the rugby codes and the rest of the country generally preferring Australian rules footy.

There's even an unofficial geographical boundary called the Barassi Line (named after the recently departed legendary Aussie rules player and coach) which separates the two distinct sporting sectors.

Never mind that there is a degree of cultural and sporting overlap, with Sydney's two AFL teams usually performing well, and the Melbourne Storm being the NRL's most consistent team for at least two decades. And never mind that the advent of first pay TV and then streaming services brought all codes to a national audience. Despite growing pockets of fans and the odd successful team implanted in enemy territory, Australia is still virtually two sporting nations in the cooler months before cricket again unites us in summer. What other country has anything like this? Imagine if half of America had no idea who Tom Brady was? Imagine if half of England had never heard of David Beckham?

Fortunately, I grew up in Canberra. Now, those might be words to make many Australians scoff, but the national capital, which by most accounts owes its name to an Aboriginal word for 'meeting place', was indeed a meeting place for the sporting codes in my childhood. It still is. To this day, Canberra has strong local competitions in Aussie rules footy, rugby league and rugby union, not to mention numerous other sports. Back in the eighties, Canberra had only one commercial TV network – Seven – and it covered the Aussie rules on Saturdays and the rugby league on Sundays. Few other Australians enjoyed the luxury of being able to watch the elite level of both codes on TV, or the luxury of being able to play your preferred sport in a local competition.

Later in life, my ingrained knowledge of the three main winter codes was like a superpower. Working on a national sports magazine, I was always catching errors that only a sporting polyglot would notice. For example, a Sydney-based journalist writing about the AFL might have used the word 'kick-off' for the start of an AFL game when it is the 'bounce', or 'referee' instead of 'umpire', or 'siren' instead of 'hooter'. Or a Melbourne-based writer mentioning the NRL might have referred to the 'tribunal' instead of the 'judiciary', or a 'free kick' instead of a 'penalty', or the 'Rabbits' instead of the 'Rabbitohs'.

For those from one of the so-called AFL states who have always wondered about the Rabbitohs, the unusual team name refers to men who used to sell rabbits for meat in the early 1900s, shouting 'Rabbit-oh' to attract business. The club's part-owner Russell Crowe apparently spends half his time in Hollywood explaining this to Americans.

Great Aussie sporting terms: *Punter*

A punter is a gambler in both British and Australian English. It can also mean a patron at the races or any event beyond the racecourse.

It can even mean a member of the masses who's not actually attending anything. But there's a subtle difference between the British and Australian uses of the word: to be a punter in the UK in the context of gambling has a slightly seedy connotation. Here, not so much.

That is not to say that punting is never seedy in this country. Gambling is a disease that ruins lives and relationships, and Australians spend more on the punt per person than any other country, averaging a loss of more than a thousand dollars a year per adult.

Nonetheless, there is a softer sense to the word in Australian culture. It taps into our innate sense of optimism – however misguided – that the average person can come out on top. To be a punter in Australia is not a byword for failure; it simply means you enjoy the occasional dabble with the winds of chance, and if you're able to keep your worst impulses under control, that is far from a terrible thing.

On a purely linguistic level, the word 'punter' is an infinitely more practical term than the American word 'bettor'. In America, a bettor bets a horse. That's just clumsy. In Australia, a punter bets *on* a horse or more commonly backs a horse. The verb 'to back' is another great sporting word. It suggests you're getting on the back of a horse, riding it as though you're the jockey, doing everything to ensure your investment comes to fruition. The word 'backing' suggests a certain emotional attachment to your wager, even if fleeting. And Australians can get emotional about racing, whether the naysayers like it or not.

By the way, if there's a better word for someone who doesn't like horse racing than 'naysayer', then we haven't heard it.

Great Aussie sporting terms: *Code*

Only Australians use this word to differentiate between sports, though the word often only refers to the various types of footy. For example, we might ask a new acquaintance which footy code they follow. But sometimes the word refers to the full panoply of team sports, including netball and hockey and soccer and whatever else.

When News Corp launched a premium subscription-only sporting website and app designed to showcase the best Australian sports writing, they called it *CODE Sports*. You might say the name is a code that all sports lovers would understand.

Spectacular Aussie sporting names: *Ariarne Titmus*

Ariarne is a Latin variation of the Greek name Ariadne, while the surname Titmus appears to be a variant of titmouse, a small chirpy northern hemisphere woodland bird. The combination sounds like the hero of a dystopian novel. Titmus, an Olympic champion in the 200m and 400m freestyle, is usually just 'Arnie' – the perfect nickname for a swimmer who has terminated too many rivals to count in winning four Olympic gold medals, three silver and a bronze in her career to date.

Great Aussie sporting terms: *Bathurst*

There are plenty of famous stadiums and venues in the world of sport, but only a select few cities, towns or suburbs are synonymous

ORNAMENT TO THE GAME

There's an old saying that no player is bigger than the game. Indeed, even when you get so big that you are almost synonymous with the game, you swell in stature but metaphorically shrink in size and become 'an ornament to the game'. Linguists will tell you that the phrase was originally 'an adornment to the game' but sometimes getting stuff wrong is a blessing, not a curse, and the phrase works perfectly as it is. If any individual in any sport was an ornament to the game in the sense that the combination of their personality and talent made the game itself greater, it was tennis legend Roger Federer.

with the sport played there. Think Wimbledon, the London suburb where the famous tennis tournament is held each summer at a venue which is actually called the All England Lawn Tennis & Croquet Club. Or Augusta, the small city in Georgia which serves as a stand-in title for golf's Masters tournament, which is played at the Augusta National Golf Club each April.

In Australia, the placename that instantly brings to mind a famous sporting event is Bathurst, in honour of the 1000-kilometre Supercars event conducted at the Mt Panorama circuit on the fringe of town each October. The official name of the race has changed several times over the years and is currently officially the Bathurst 1000. But everyone just calls it Bathurst. And Bathurst means so much more than the race.

It means camping on top of the mountain

at McPhillamy Park, where the thing to do at night in race week is throw burning toilet rolls. Why? Because Bathurst! It means donuts and burnouts in car parks. Why? Because Bathurst! It means searing heat and freezing cold that can even bring spring snowfalls. Why? Because Bathurst! It means signs proclaiming undying loyalty to car manufacturers who thumbed their noses at Australian workers and their families by pulling out of local manufacturing. Why? Because Bathurst!

I covered one – and only one – Bathurst in my time as a writer for a national sports magazine. This was back in the 2000s. After practice one day, I hitched a ride back into town with one of the drivers in his own car. I can't remember what he drove, but I'll never forget he detoured out on a quiet country dirt road and pulled donuts like a teenage hoon. Was I scared? Absolutely. Was I excited? Yes, although the fear factor mitigated the excitement. Was I surprised? Even more so.

Drivers these days are pretty refined characters. To get the big contracts, you've got to present yourself as a serious professional, more like an accountant than a delinquent. Gone are the days when a wild young petrolhead could rise through the ranks – and it should be mentioned that 'petrolhead' is another great Australian sporting word.

Anyway, this bloke was still a bit of a wild boy at heart. He loved pushing any vehicle to its limits, and since we were on a quiet road in the middle of nowhere and could hurt nobody but ourselves, pulling a few dusty donuts wasn't the worst thing that had ever happened. Professionalism wins titles, but where would sport be without passion?

That young driver got on the podium in that year's race too. Sorry, but his identity must remain a secret. Check the placegetters of all Bathursts in the 2000s – and I'm not telling you if he was the lead driver or the co-driver – and take your best guess. Anyway, the point of the story is that it was all very, very Bathurst.

Great Aussie sporting terms: *The ladder*

'The ladder' is the updated week-to-week rankings of teams in any sporting league, from most games won to least. Most countries use 'table' while Americans tend to use 'standings' and South Africans sometimes use the word 'logs'. But we have a 'ladder', and apart from it being a really fun word, you could argue that it speaks to our ingrained sense of egalitarianism. In our careers, we tend to find a place on the corporate ladder, with only a few of us ascending to the top. But sport resets each year. With sporting ladders, there is fresh hope with each year that our team will reach the top rung.

Great Aussie sporting terms: *Biffo*

One of the most prized items in my backyard writer's shed is a can of KB Lager signed by three rugby league giants: Andrew Johns, Matty Johns and Reg Reagan.

Andrew is one of just fourteen Immortals, the game's highest honour. Matty is his brother, who was good enough to play for his state and country. And Reagan was Matty Johns's alter ego, whose beverage of choice was the old-school New South Wales beer KB Lager, and whose famous catchphrase was 'Bring back the biff' – a deliciously non-PC lament for the days before multiple TV cameras, when rugby league was basically a boxing match on grass.

'Biff', and its sibling 'biffo', are words unique to Australia and New Zealand, both meaning fighting or a fight. English language thesauruses have a big chunk of a page devoted to words and short phrases meaning fight. Some of them include:

> brouhaha, melee, fracas, ruckus, fisticuffs,
> imbroglio, barney, donnybrook, set-to,
> contretemps, punch-up, scrap, altercation,
> tiff, stoush, rumble, scrap, tete a tete,
> affray, brannigan, brawl, argy bargy, tussle,
> exchange of blows, dust-up, stink, blue,
> Larry Dooley.

Of those terms mentioned, 'stink', 'blue', 'biffo' and 'Larry Dooley' are probably the most

SELECTION HEADACHE

There are good selection headaches and bad selection headaches. Good ones are when a coach has so many players in form, they'll agonise over who to squeeze into the team. A bad selection headache is when half the team is injured or suspended or hopelessly out of form and they just can't work out how they'll cobble together a team for the weekend. Whatever the case, it's time to reach for the strongest painkiller in the team first aid kit.

Australian. But biffo is the best and we should never let the word die, even if the biff was never brought back and remains banned in all rugby league competitions.

Great Aussie sporting quirks: *National team names*

How good were the Matildas in the 2023 FIFA Women's World Cup? You've probably forgotten that Spain won the tournament after beating England in the final, or that Australia finished fourth after losing to Sweden in the playoff for third. But who cares?

In terms of public interest, the Matildas were the winners, generating the biggest TV audience ever recorded in Australia – and not just for sport, but for anything. Eleven million people tuned in to the semi-final against

England at the peak of the broadcast. That's almost half the country.

Why the zeitgeist? Why did the Matildas so captivate the nation? A huge and obvious part of the story is the long overdue rise of women's professional team sport as fodder for television. But the Matildas have become a brand, and a huge part of that brand is their name, which dates back to 1994, when the Australian national women's football team qualified for their first World Cup. They were then known as the Female Socceroos (with the men's team nicknamed the Socceroos), but broadcaster SBS and the now defunct Australian Women's Soccer Association thought they could do better, so they ran a phone poll with choices which included: Soccertoos, Blue Flyers, Waratahs, Matildas and Lorikeets.

Soccertoos? *Really*?

Fortunately, the wise people of Australia picked up their landlines with their curly-wurly phone cords and voted for the Matildas. And today, the worm has totally turned to the point where former Socceroo Craig Foster jokingly calls himself a former 'Mantilda'.

The Matildas are just one of many cherished names for Australian national sporting teams. Most countries don't do this. While there are a few notable exceptions, like South African rugby's Springboks or England's Lionesses (who beat the Matildas 3–1 in that World Cup semi-final), team nicknames tend to be reserved for competitions between sporting clubs or 'franchises', as they're often called now.

Play for America in any sport and you're part of 'Team USA'. Boooriiing. But if you play for Australia in hockey, you're a Hockeyroo (women) or a Kookaburra (men). Play in rugby league and you're a Kangaroo (men) or a Jillaroo (women). Rugby union has the Wallabies (men) and the Wallaroos (women). Our netballers are Diamonds, our women's basketballers are Opals and our men's basketballers are Boomers. There are dozens of others.

The only other country that has nicknames for most of their national teams is New Zealand, and because their most famous international team is their men's rugby team, aka the All Blacks, most of the teams are the Black Somethings or Something Black. So the cricketers are the Black Caps, the men's basketballers are the amusingly named Tall Blacks, and so on. The really funny one was the New Zealand men's badminton team. Can you guess it? Obviously, you hit a shuttlecock in badminton, so for a while there in 2004, the team called themselves ... wait for it ... the Black Cocks. (Yes, they really did.) According to the *Te Ara Encyclopedia of New Zealand*, 'There was immediate sponsorship interest from condom companies, but the name drew ridicule from the public and firm opposition from the International Badminton Federation. It was soon officially dropped.'

Yes, the *Encyclopedia of New Zealand* really mentions 'firm opposition' to the name Black Cocks.

On a more family-orientated note and back here across the Ditch in Australia, there are two very prominent teams which break the rule – the men's and women's national cricket teams. The men have never had a nickname. Because of their prominence and immense popularity, perhaps it's their way of staying above the pack. The women had a nickname for a while – the Southern Stars – but abandoned it in 2017. Perhaps that was their way of saying that female athletes were no less important than the men.

Not that anyone needs to be told that after the success of the Matildas.

Great Aussie sporting terms: *To do a Bradbury*

We all know the story of Steven Bradbury, the Aussie who won gold in the 1000 metre short track speed skating at the Salt Lake 2002 Winter Olympics. The Queenslander trailed the four leaders by the best part of half a lap in the nine-lap final, then watched as they crashed into each other on the home turn, leaving him free to glide across the line in first place.

The look on Bradbury's face as he crossed the line was priceless: elation mixed with shock. There was a lot going through his head in that moment and its immediate aftermath, to the point where he almost couldn't bear to make his way out to the podium when it was time to accept Australia's first ever Winter Olympic gold medal.

'After I had a few quiet moments to myself, I decided I'd take the medal, not for that race itself, but for the fourteen years of hard work in the lead-up to that race,' Bradbury told me in a 2018 interview for the *AthletesVoice* website.

'I guess really, there was no choice, there was nowhere else to go. But it didn't sit comfortably with me at that point, and if you see me at the medal ceremony, you can see that.

'But all of those feelings were pretty quickly diminished when they started to play the Aussie national anthem, and there were 16,000 people in that stadium. For me, it didn't feel like there was anybody else there, and that was when I was really able to enjoy the gold medal for the first time.'

Today, Bradbury has come to love that moment. He says the hairs on the back of his neck stand up every time he watches the replay of that chaotic final lap. Which Australian doesn't feel the same? To this day, the phrase 'to do a Bradbury' means to triumph from an impossible position in any sport. But the phrase deserves to convey a richer meaning.

A little-remembered fact about Bradbury is that he was actually a world class athlete earlier in his career. Indeed, he was part of the relay team that won Australia's first Winter Olympic medal of any colour, a bronze in the 5000 metre relay at the 1994 Winter Olympics in Lillehammer, Norway. Later that year, he suffered an horrific injury in a World Cup race when another skater's blade sliced through all four quadriceps on his right thigh. He lost four litres of blood and rehab took almost two years. Cut forward to 2002, and Bradbury was nowhere near the athlete he once was, but he had experience on his side. Another little-known fact is that the events of the Salt Lake Olympic final were a near replica of the semi-final, when Bradbury also hung off the pace and was the beneficiary of a pile-up that didn't involve him.

Doing a Bradbury? It means being the recipient of outrageous fortune, but it could just as well stand for resilience and smarts. Because Steven Bradbury wouldn't have won his famous gold medal without both of those qualities. A huge dollop of luck was the icing on the cake – or, in his case, the caking on the ice.

Great Aussie sporting terms: *Trust the process*

This is the only term in this book that I really hate. Once upon a time, sport gave the corporate world many of its best words and phrases. As the language of the dressing room infiltrated the boardroom, phrases like 'knock it out of the park', 'the ball is in your court', 'gamechanger', 'call the shots', 'par for the course', 'touch base', 'it's a marathon, not a sprint' and 'teamwork makes the dream work' became part of everyday office language.

Times have changed. As the landscape of Australia's professional sports has become increasingly corporatised, and as most players are put through some sort of media training, bland management terminology has increasingly worked its way into the mouths of athletes. 'Yeah, we just trusted our process,' players will now say in post-match interviews after a win.

It'd be nice if they shifted the goalposts – so to speak – back to the days when players said, 'We were on fire out there today' or 'We just wanted it more'. Sport is one of the few real, unscripted things left in the world and it'd be nice to see players talk about the emotion and vibe rather than describing it with a phrase that sounds like the motto of a business school.

Spectacular Aussie sporting names: *Layne Beachley*

Some athletes were just born to play the game. When your surname has the word 'beach' in it and you grew up around the famous Sydney beachside suburb of Manly, it's fate that you'd become a seven-time world surfing champion rather than, say, an alpine ski racer.

INJURY TOLL

When a team has a high 'injury toll', it means a high tally or total, as that's one meaning of the word 'toll'. But a toll is of course also a word for a fee, and the cliche works in that sense too. Success in sport is often a case of luck, timing and good management – and managing injuries is a big part of that. If you've got too many good players injured, well, you'll pay the toll.

Of course, there was also a famous alpine ski racer born in Manly – the lawyer, climate change activist, politician and 1998 Winter Olympic bronze medallist in slalom Zali Steggall. Zali is a pretty cool name too (and her Olympic snowboarder brother is called Zeke, so the Steggall parents clearly had a bit of a thing for Zs).

But back to Beachley, she's a seven-time world champion, a member of the Surfers' Hall of Fame, and she has even voiced a surfing character in *Bluey,* which is when you really know you've made it in life.

Great Aussie sporting terms: *Sledge*

Where would we be without the word 'sledge'? And how do other countries cope without a specific word that means to abuse a rival player on the field?

Sledges are usually flung in good-natured tones, although things can turn ugly when they get personal. The most famous sporting sledge in Australian sporting history is the 'Can't bowl, can't throw' comment from a teammate in reference to Australian cricket team rookie Scott Muller, who wasn't having a great time of things in his second (and, as it turns out, final) Test match at Hobart in 1999. The sledge was picked up on the stump mic and nationwide speculation raged as to the identity of the sledger. It continues to this day.

Nine cameraman Joe Privatera eventually came forward and took the fall, but no one has ever seriously believed it was him. Most still believe it had to be a player nearby. Mark Waugh and Adam Gilchrist are prime candidates, as both were close to the stumps. Shane Warne was one name often put forward because it seemed like a totally Shane Warne thing to do. If he did say it, the truth is sadly buried with him.

Then again, maybe the truth can still be unearthed. In 2006, Muller broke his silence in the magazine *Inside Cricket*. He didn't give much away but he did say, 'There's a certain umpire out there who knows what really happened.' The umpires that day were the Englishman Peter Willey and the Australian Peter Parker. Both gentlemen are still very much alive, so perhaps one day one of them will enlighten us all.

As for the origins of the word 'sledge', the Australian National University's School of Literature, Languages and Linguistics says that the word was first recorded in the 1970s in the cricketing context. In the 1990s, veteran Sydney journalist and former rugby league coach Roy Masters wrote a story about how the word ended up in cricket. Long story short, during a party in a motel room midway through a match in the mid-1960s, a player swore in front of a woman and someone told him he was as subtle as a sledgehammer.

From that moment on, in Australian cricketing circles, someone who swore in front of a woman became known as a 'sledge' (or sometimes as a 'Percy', named for American singer Percy Sledge, who recorded the soul classic 'When a Man Loves a Woman' in 1966). The term evolved to mean anyone who insulted someone at any time, then, like an out-of-control bushfire, it jumped the containment lines of cricket to other sports and to all facets of Australian life.

As for Australian sport's cleverest sledge, there are too many to list, but perhaps the greatest sledge ever levelled at an Australian was directed at none other than Shane Warne, who was never far from the sledging action. On this occasion, however, the sledge came from an unlikely source. Daryll Cullinan was a fine South African batter who averaged a very respectable 44.21 across his Test career but a woeful 12.75 against Australia. Indeed, in thirteen innings against Australia, he never reached 50. The reason? He was Shane Warne's bunny. (And bunny, by the way, is a great cricket word even if it's not exclusively Aussie. It refers to a batter who always gets dismissed by the same bowler whereas a 'rabbit', more broadly, just means a hopeless batter.)

As for Daryll Cullinan, the poor bloke just could not deal with Warne. But in the first Test at Johannesburg in 1997, it was more than three years since the two had met at cricket's highest level, and the theory – in the South African camp at least – was that things would be different. Suffice to say that Warne thought otherwise.

'I've been waiting four years for an opportunity to get you again,' Warne told his hapless foe.

'Looks like you spent it eating,' Cullinan said.

Oof! Bam! Thwok! But the verbal blow was only a flesh wound, excuse the pun. Warne had his revenge on the field, dismissing Cullinan for a duck in the second innings as Australia won that first Test en route to a series win.

Great Aussie sporting terms: *Blinder*

To 'play a blinder' means to go out there and have an absolute belter, a cracker, a ripsnorter, a humdinger, an absolute beauty. Interestingly, 'blinders' is the American term for what Australians call 'blinkers', as in the cups made of plastic or leather which deliberately restrict a horse's peripheral vision. These are often used to calm horses and to keep them focused on their task. But in Australia where the term is widely used, and in the UK where it quite likely originated, if several players have blinders, it's a safe bet your team will have dominated the opposition. Presumably the term has similar origins to the word 'dazzling', as in someone so brilliant that watching them is a bit like staring at the sun.

Great Aussie sporting terms: *Go the tonk*

To tonk the ball in Australian cricket parlance is to whack it, usually in an unorthodox manner. But to go the tonk entails an entire change of mindset. At some point in your innings, probably because of a match situation where rapid run-scoring is required, it's time to make the switch, like powering up in a video game. It's time to go the tonk. Fours and sixes are the only goal at this point. Occupation of the crease serves no other purpose. In the book *Warwick Todd goes the Tonk* by TV personality and author Tom Gleisner, going the tonk serves as a metaphor for being behaviourally unhinged. So it goes at the batting crease.

Interestingly, many words like 'tonk' that Australians have generously donated to world cricket have been most enthusiastically adopted by Indian fans. The world's leading cricket website, espncricinfo.com, has a real-time, ball-by-ball commentary for every professional match played anywhere in the world, usually written by Indian writers. Many Indians writing in English, whether on sport or other subjects, still tend to use old-fashioned English words that were commonplace in the literature of the Raj (the period when Britain ruled the Indian subcontinent, from 1858 to 1947). But they'll combine old-school terminology with newfangled Aussie cricket words.

For example, on the live commentary for an IPL match in the 2024 season in which Aussie batter Travis Head was smashing them all over the park, the writer used the delicious phrase 'preposterous tonking!'. And that was not the only combination of old and new words in his copy. There was 'thrashes merrily', 'spanked with insolence' and my favourite, 'jauntily hoicked'.

'Hoicked' is another great Aussie cricket word, meaning to hit the ball in a somewhat ungainly manner. You can just about smell the Aerogard and taste the sizzling sausages when you hear the word. But to see it prefaced with the very un-Australian word 'jauntily', well, it was preposterous!

Great Aussie sporting terms: *Fixture*

The AFL has a unique relationship with the word 'fixture', using the term to mean not just one match, but the entire season's schedule.

In the wider world, and in most parts of Australia, a fixture means a single sporting event or match. When referring to an entire season's worth of matches, you might use

INJURY CLOUD

I have always loved this cliche, which refers to a player who may or may not be ready to play in an upcoming match depending on the severity of their injury and whether it heals in time. Whenever I try to picture it, I am reminded of a cartoon character who has a black cloud hovering over them wherever they go. It never occurred to me that the cloud itself might be injured!

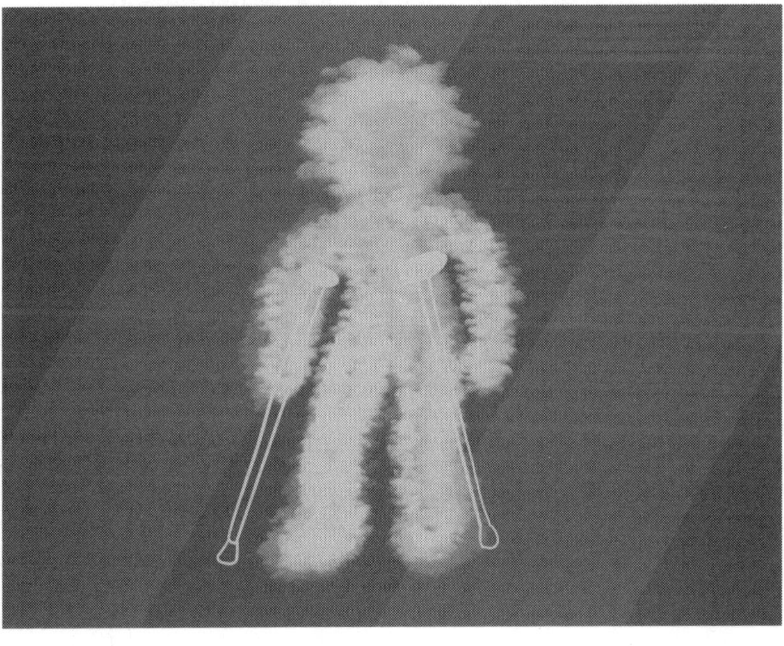

the word fixtures (plural) but never fixture (singular). The English Premier League website has a tab marked 'fixtures' where you can view all the matches in the season ahead, as does Australia's A-League. Other codes here use an assortment of words. The NRL uses the term 'draw', the NBL uses 'schedule' in the American tradition, while Cricket Australia simply has a 'matches' tab on its website.

Interestingly, Cricket Australia's website used to have the word 'fixture' for the entire summer of cricket but appears to have abandoned the term. Why? Well, Cricket Australia's headquarters is literally across the road from the MCG, so its culture resembles that of the AFL in many ways. Did it adopt the AFL term 'fixture' for multiple matches not realising most Australian sports don't use it that way? Almost certainly. Did someone tap

CA on the shoulder and say, 'No one in any other state knows what the hell you're talkin' about?' Probably.

The main other sporting league in Australia that uses the word fixture to mean all upcoming games is Super Netball. It is surely no coincidence that Netball Australia is based in Melbourne.

Great Aussie sporting terms: *Bradmanesque*

There was only one Don Bradman and the great batter remains a byword for Australian sporting excellence. How many elite individuals, in any field, become an adjective? To be Bradmanesque in Australian sport means that you're putting huge numbers on the board, or stringing together an incredible run of success. There is no higher praise.

Fun Bradman fact: the ABC's post office box in each capital city is PO Box 9994 – an obvious reference to The Don's Test batting average of 99.94. His average remains a remarkable statistical outlier as the next clump of players on the list all have averages in the 60s. Comb through statistics in any sport in any country and you won't find anything close to Bradman's dominance over his nearest rivals; not in the goals of Messi, the Grand Slam titles of Margaret Court, the tally of Tiger Woods's golf tournament victories – nowhere.

Bradman's dominance drives Indian cricket fans mad. They argue that their man, Sachin Tendulkar, was greater because he scored 15,921 runs to Bradman's 6996. But the diminutive Indian batted 329 times in Tests compared to Bradman's eighty, which means he played more than four times as many innings, yet only scored a little over double the runs. That's reflected in Tendulkar's career Test average of 53.78.

Indians also argue that Bradman never excelled in abbreviated forms of the game as Tendulkar did, racking up forty-nine One Day International centuries to go with his fifty-one in Tests for an unprecedented total of one hundred hundreds in international cricket. But white-ball cricket had not been invented in Bradman's day, so who knows how many runs he would have scored in that format?

Also worth noting is that Bradman travelled by ship to play in England, which surely must have made it hard to retain fitness and form. Yet he averaged 102.84 in nineteen Tests in that country. Lastly, pitches were uncovered in those days, meaning the surface was much less predictable, consistent or friendly for batting.

Case closed. Sachin Tendulkar was not even remotely Bradmanesque. And if someone in Australian sport is described as Bradmanesque, you know they're experiencing a remarkable run of form – even if their overall career stats are extremely unlikely to match those of The Don.

Spectacular Aussie sporting names: *Matt Hilder*

Matt Hilder had a successful NRL career playing for three clubs between 2003 and 2013.

'But wait,' you say. 'Matt Hilder is not an unusual or exotic name!'

Not by itself, no. But try it with his nickname 'Waltzing' before it.

Great Aussie sporting terms: *Clanger*

'Clanger' is a well-established word in British English, but it took us Aussies to turn it into an official word in Aussie rules footy. Champion Data, the company that has been the official statistical data provider to the AFL since 1999, defines it as 'an error made by a player resulting in a negative result for their side'. That's the official definition, but in the minds of fans, a clanger means any dumb or clumsy moment of play. With clangers, it's a case of you know one when you see one. Watching the game, did you just inadvertently bury your face in your hands in dismay? That's because you saw a clanger.

The word is occasionally used in everyday life too. 'Can you believe it? Alex bought a coffee and spilled it on their shirt right before the meeting with a key client. What a clanger!'

Great Aussie sporting terms: *Spray*

'Spray' is a uniquely Australian term for angry words directed at another person, usually in sport and usually toward players by a captain or, more commonly, a coach. Presumably the word derives from the sprinkling of saliva that inadvertently accompanies such an outburst.

There have been many infamous coaching sprays in professional sport over the years, but perhaps the most vitriolic Aussie coaching spray was delivered in suburban Aussie rules footy in Melbourne around 2010, after a local team was up by 70 at half-time and proceeded to lose by 3 points. It's out there on YouTube and it occupies a space somewhere between downright nasty and absolutely hilarious.

'Was it seventy points we were up by at

half-time? Seventy points? Yeah. We've lost by three. Go and f--k yourselves, fellas!'

That's how it begins and it's not the most encouraging start to a post-match spray.

'I could rant and rave. I could rant and rave but I realised today that I am coaching a s--t football team.'

More ruthless belittlement, but at least it seemed like the coach was going to end his spray there without turning it into a prolonged rant. Turns out, he was just warming up. We won't print the speech in full, but parts of it include (extremely loud yelling in bold):

'Physically, I don't think we're there. Mentally, I don't think we're there. And it's **doing my f--ken head in!** I put the f--ken time in each week ... I get bananas, I get lollies, I get Solo ... **shove the fu--ken Solo up your arse!**

Seriously! Don't open the can. Shove it up your f--ken arse!'

It gets worse. You might wonder how it could, but it does. Unspeakable acts are suggested before it ends with the coach once more exhorting the players to go f--k themselves.

In amateur sport these days, and especially in junior sport, the culture is to be overwhelmingly inclusive and encouraging toward even the lazy and/or untalented players. You'd be banned for life for giving a speech like that. And while you might argue that the 'every child wins a prize' mentality compromises the inherently competitive nature of sport, it's surely a good thing that expletive-riddled sprays are no longer commonplace.

For the grown-ups, though, there's still room for a good old-fashioned spray. But maybe just let the players drink their Solo rather than encouraging them to commit unspeakable acts with it.

Great Aussie sporting quirks: *Club songs*

You sing it when your team runs through the banner. You hopefully sing it at the end of the game when your team has had a glorious victory by one point over a despised rival, because a narrow victory over an arch-enemy is always so much sweeter than a blowout. Winning players sing it in the sheds (see page 98), usually horribly out of tune, but who cares? Club songs are a great Aussie rules footy tradition that is rapidly spreading to other sports.

Every once in a while, media outlets trot out their song rankings and they're always in more

PREMIERSHIP WINDOW

You've got a good team. You've got the classic blend of youth and experience (see page 20). The experienced guys aren't yet over the hill, and the young guys aren't too raw. You've got the right coach and everything is in place. This is your time. Your premiership window is open. Now if only it were as simple as reaching through that open window and grabbing that tantalising trophy...

or less the same order, with Richmond usually first and the Fremantle Dockers usually last.

This is correct, no matter which version you're talking about. Freo's song used to start with a rendition of the old Russian folk song 'Song of the Volga Boatmen'. So there was a loose stevedoring connection, although that still doesn't explain why they chose a Russian tune. Anyway, that only lasted about ten seconds before the song totally changed pace and vibe, morphing into a sort of hair-metal horror show that sounds like it was sung by the band members Bon Jovi rejected. This part is now the entire song, and it's still terrible.

An underrated newcomer is the Giants, who are on the record stating that their club song is the best in the league. And they might be right. The thing about club songs is that the classic ones, like Richmond and Carlton and Collingwood, all sound like show tunes from the golden age of musicals. The Giants' song, 'There's a Big, Big Sound', captures that vibe perfectly, with a catchy toe-tapping oompah beat holding it all together.

The song was written by Harry Angus of Australian jazz/funk band The Cat Empire. The Giants' inaugural coach, Kevin Sheedy, reckoned the new Giants song needed a moment that replicated the moment in the Richmond song where fans and players shout the words 'yellow and black'. In the Giants song, the words 'never surrender' do exactly that. It's the moment when singing turns to raw shouting, although anyone who's ever watched any team sing any club song could argue that the shouting pretty much starts from the first line!

Anyway, the Giants' song is a beauty. Angry Anderson said it needed more guitar, but

Harry Angus made the excellent point that the songs with electric guitar date really quickly (hi, Freo!), whereas the ones with the classic vibe stay fresh forever.

The only other point worth making here is that real tigers are orange and black, not yellow and black, like the Richmond team jerseys or the famous line in their song. I googled this to check and the top hit was an old story on the subject written by none other than myself. (It's amazing how you can forget about a story you wrote.) Anyway, in the story I actually interviewed someone from the World Wildlife Fund and they confirmed that yes indeed, tigers are orange. Bengal tigers, Sumatran tigers, Siberian tigers, South China tigers, Malayan tigers, the Wests Tigers, any tigers you can think of – all of them orange.

Great Aussie sporting terms: *Flat-track bully*

A flat-track bully is a person who is super competent when they're in their comfort zone, but wilts when the heat turns up. They're the person who totally fails to get going when the going gets tough. You'd never, ever call anyone a flat-track bully to their face, but it's a useful phrase which has eked its way into the general Australian consciousness beyond the sporting field.

Queensland opening batter Matthew Hayden was your classic flat-track bully. Give him a nice hard domestic wicket and he'd bat all day, and most of the next too.

Put the giant Queenslander on a tricky pitch against tough opposition and forget it. This was the theory early in his career, anyway. And to be fair, it was pretty accurate at the time.

But after a couple of false starts in the baggy green, Haydos eventually cemented his place at the top of the order, playing 103 Tests at the phenomenal average of 50.73 for an opening batter. So, it turns out, he wasn't a flat-track bully after all. But you get the idea.

Great Aussie sporting terms: *Thrashing*

If you ever needed proof that Australia had a convict past, look no further than the words 'thrashing' and 'flogging', both of which originate from the act of whipping someone, but when applied in a sporting context refer to a team or player beating an opponent by a huge margin.

In recent years, the word 'flog' has taken on a secondary, less savoury meaning. Calling someone a flog infers that they spend too much time flogging, an act almost always done in private. That's doubtless why you don't see the word 'flogging' in too many headlines anymore. But we still speak of 'a thrashing' or a match in which your team 'thrashed' the opposition, and when you come home from the game half-tanked on half-strength beer, it's one of those really satisfying words to say.

Spectacular Aussie sporting names: *The Nunawading Spectres*

I grew up watching the Canberra Cannons back in the days when they were winning titles in the National Basketball League (NBL). The Cannons are now defunct, and so too are all but two of the original teams from the league's inaugural season in 1979. One of the extinct foundation teams was called the Nunawading Spectres. That was also the name of a team in the Women's National Basketball League that won six championships in its ten seasons of existence from 1982 to 1991.

Nunawading is a suburb in Melbourne's east whose name is said to mean a battlefield or ceremonial ground in the Woi Wurrung language of the Wurundjeri people. A spectre is of course a particularly cool name for a ghost or spirit. Together, the two words are veritable verbal velvet. The Nunawading Spectres. Once you start saying it, you can't stop.

When in 1987 the men's team changed its name to the Eastside Spectres (presumably to broaden its appeal within Melbourne beyond the suburb of Nunawading), it was the beginning of the end. But like an apparition, the name has returned! The Nunawading Spectres now compete in both the men's and women's NBL1 South, a semi-professional league that sits below the NBL.

Great Aussie sporting terms: *Avagoyamug!*

This old cricket crowd favourite is little heard these days, but there are still those who remember times when beer was full strength in the outer and sunscreen and shirts (for blokes, at least) were optional. During a quiet patch in play, someone would yell, 'Avagoyamug' as in 'Have a go, you mug', which meant 'Come on, mate, we're bored, hit the bloody ball for six, or at least try!'

Used mostly in cricket, the phrase was typically directed the way of stodgy England opening batters, but would occasionally be turned on a member of the home team. Australian sports fans love their team to win,

GAME FACE

If you've got your game face on, you're looking serious. No more joking around in the 'sheds' (see page 98). It's all about business now. When you think about it, 'game face' is a pretty funny expression – especially if taken literally!

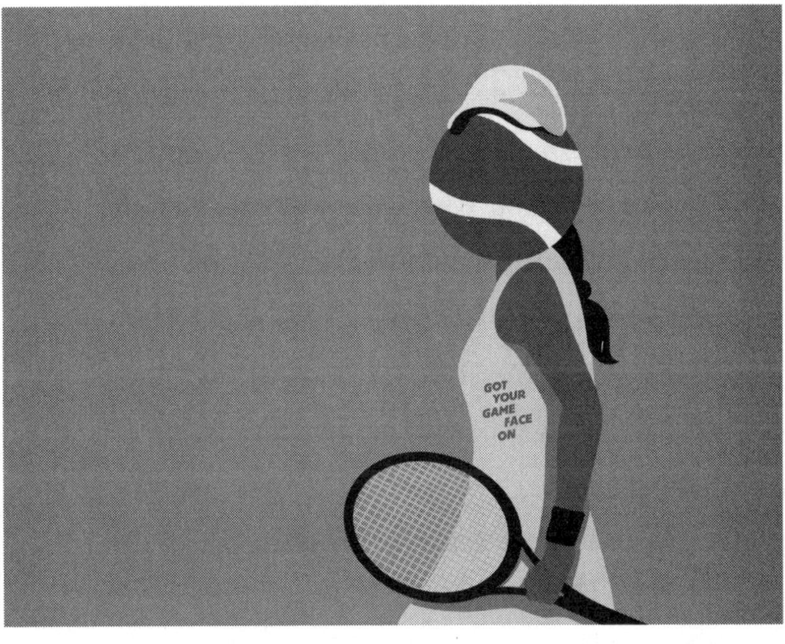

but we like to be entertained too. Grinding out tough, unspectacular victories is necessary at times in any sport, but it has never been the Australian strategy of choice.

There are quite a few Aussie sporting terms which are portmanteaux of several other words. 'Getadogupya' comes to mind, although perhaps that one is not suitable for work. Another example in the various footy codes is 'Chewyonyaboot' which you yell at someone lining up a kick for goal. Strangely, in all my years of attending sport of all kinds, I have never once seen a player react to this cry by checking if they do indeed have chewing gum on their boot.

Great Aussie sporting terms: *The sheds*

All professional sport in Australia owes much to bush sport, where so many legendary careers are forged. And what are the main facilities in bush sport? Usually a shed. American sport has these you-beaut pathways for young athletes, where the bells and whistles and facilities of professional sport are replicated at college and even high-school level. It's safe to say that few NFL players ever got changed in a shed from the time they started taking American football seriously as teenagers. But in the towns and suburbs of Australia, for budding athletes of all ages and ability levels, sheds it is, with quartered oranges at half-time and a burnt sausage on a piece of unbuttered white bread afterwards, if you're lucky.

As mentioned in the intro to this book, occasionally the sheds are given fancy grandiose names like 'the inner sanctum', but that's usually TV commentators trying to add a touch of drama. Ask any Australian professional sportsperson and they'll say 'sheds'. Why do we say sheds, plural? Because we just do. And sometimes, that answer is enough.

Great Aussie sporting terms: *Meat pie and sausage roll*

These are not only foods you eat in the stands, if indeed you can classify them as 'food'. Australia's favourite sporting snacks also happen to be rhyming slang for the main points-scoring objectives in our two most popular winter codes.

A try in rugby league is a 'meat pie' and a goal in Aussie rules footy is a 'sausage roll'. And if you are actually eating those foods at the footy, don't forget the dead horse (sauce) or the Britney Spears (beers).

The concept of rhyming slang is a British cockney tradition which has been adopted enthusiastically on these shores, and there are many other examples relevant to Australian sport. Your favourite player's having a shocker? No, they're not, they're having a Barry, as in a Barry Crocker, a veteran Australian actor. In parts of the country, it's common to refer to spare change as 'Kembla', as in Kembla Grange, the racecourse in the city of Wollongong.

Even some players' surnames have become rhyming slang, although often not in a good way. Essendon champ James Hird is rhyming slang for something you can't polish. And you really don't want to know what the old VFL footballer turned media personality Rex Hunt stands for.

Oddly, there are even a couple of sporting personalities whose names substitute for the illicit drug ecstasy. One is Gary Ablett (both Senior and Junior), because the name rhymes with tablet. The other is slightly more obscure.

Ecstasy is often shortened to 'eccy', so some Victorians call the drug 'Dan Mielicki' after the race caller (whose surname is usually pronounced 'Milecky') who called thirteen Melbourne Cups but is now regarded as the nation's finest harness racing caller.

Speaking of harness racing, aka 'the trots', that sport has its own piece of rhyming slang which works on two levels. The term 'red hots' is first and foremost a rhyme with trots, but it also subtly refers to the fact that some of the sport's races in its distant, less-regulated past were said to be 'red hot', as in fixed. Not that anything like that happens nowadays ...

Spectacular Aussie sporting names: *The Great White Shark*

Australia's greatest ever golfer, Greg Norman, earned his famous nickname at the 1981

Masters, which he led early. After telling a local reporter that he grew up swimming with great white sharks, the *Atlanta Constitution* ran a headline the next day referring to him as 'Great White Shark' rather than Norman. The Shark (as he is also known in Australia because even nicknames must often be abbreviated here) said it was the best thing anyone in the media ever did for him.

What's less well known is that an Australian did the same favour for Jack Nicklaus, the man who has won more golf majors than any other. Watching Nicklaus play in Australia early in his career, Melbourne sportswriter Don Lawrence said he looked like a 'cuddly, golden bear'. Nicklaus's wife, Barbara, loved the description and the name 'The Golden Bear' stuck and became the official logo for all Jack Nicklaus merchandise.

Norman and Nicklaus are also connected in that the Shark read the Bear's golf books early in his career and built his game on Jack's, like a delightful sporting fairy tale. But there's one sense in which they'll never be mentioned in the same breath, and that's their record in golf's four major tournaments. As mentioned, Nicklaus holds the record, with 18. Tiger Woods is second with 15. Norman won just two British Opens seven years apart, and while he spent a total of 331 weeks as world number one (second behind only Tiger Woods), he was known for choking on the last day of majors, which doesn't sound like something a shark would do too often with all those teeth, but Norman finished runner-up in majors eight times – and it wasn't just bad luck.

Great Aussie sporting terms: *The death*

Australian racing has an interesting relationship with death.

Racetracks are rated in terms of their moisture content as fast, good, dead, slow or heavy, in that order, from driest to wettest. Why is dead the middle one? Race meetings are abandoned when the track is too heavy; surely this should be the dead rating. The race meeting is dead. Go home. The word 'dead', or 'dead 'un', also applies to a horse that is said to be not trying, not that such things ever (officially) happen in a sport as clean-cut as racing.

Australians also use the phrase 'the death' in two different sports.

The first is 'the death' in cricket, where it refers to the final few overs in One Day or

BALL MAGNET

Some players just have the knack of being where the ball is, or knowing where it is going to be and gaining multiple possessions throughout a match. We call such players ball magnets. There is no such actual thing as an actual magnet that attracts balls because most balls are not made of metal and magnetism doesn't work that way. Or does it ...?

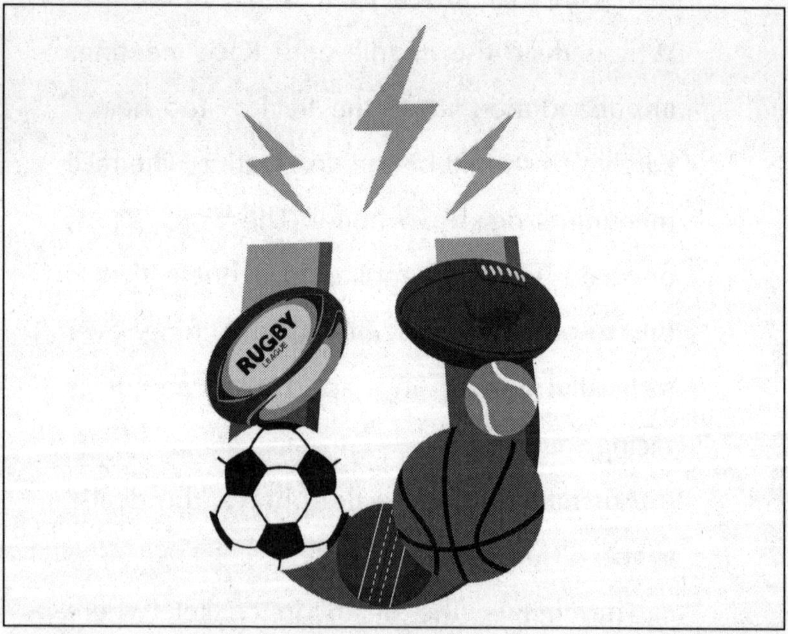

Twenty20 cricket. Bowlers who specialise in bowling during this period are known as 'death bowlers'. (If you were around in the 1980s, surely the phrase 'death bowler' brings to mind the old AIDS awareness ad, featuring the Grim Reaper playing ten-pin bowling?)

The other use of 'the death' is in harness racing, aka the trots. In that sport, it is super important to have 'cover', which means having a horse in front of you to minimise the effects of wind drag. A horse which is one out from the fence and one back from the leaders during the race is said to have the coveted 'one-one', or 'sweet seat'. The horse sitting outside the leader is said to be 'facing the breeze' or 'sitting in the death seat', or simply 'in the death'. Almost every race, the caller will say a horse has 'got the death', as though it's caught some terrible medieval illness. As any punter knows, it might as well have caught the plague because horses in the death rarely win.

Great Aussie sporting terms: *Getting around your teammates*

Back in 2018, I interviewed British netballer Jo Harten, who had just arrived in Sydney for what has turned out to be a lengthy stint at Giants Netball in the Super Netball competition. The piece ran with the headline 'Help! I'm turning into an Aussie' because much of our conversation centred around the strange dialect she'd been forced to adopt to fit into the local netball culture, which included calling netball 'netty' – because Australians have to abbreviate every word, even if you don't lose a syllable.

To her credit, Harten had picked up the local lingo quickly. She was having a great laugh during the interview as she showed off all her newly learned Aussie slang in mock sentences about her life here. She was like 'I might stop at the servo to pick up a sanga after training 'sarvo! Or maybe I'll just go to Maccas.'

The one Aussie phrase that Harten totally didn't get when she first heard it was 'get around each other'. She literally had no idea what it meant. 'Getting around your teammates' is a newish phrase in the unofficial Australian sporting dictionary. It has both a literal and a figurative meaning. It can mean supporting your teammates emotionally, for example, you get around someone whose recent form has been down on their best. But mostly it refers to the physical act of hugging your fellow players in times of celebration, like after a win or a key moment in a game. 'Getting around your teammates' suggests a certain protectiveness too. When you get around them, you are both embracing them and defending them from outsiders. It's a really positive phrase that embodies everything that's great about team sports.

Great Aussie sporting terms: *The pill*

The pill is the ball in a variety of sports. Why is the ball the pill? Because if the first rule of Australian linguistic life is that you have to abbreviate everything, and the second rule is that any noun can be a verb, then the third rule is that if you can't abbreviate a word, you must at least find a different word of equal length.

Great Aussie sporting quirks: *Footy banners*

Back in 2014, Melbourne comedian Danny McGinlay was dismayed by what he called the 'insipid' banner held up by the cheer squad of his beloved Western Bulldogs before a game. So he contacted the club, who told him if he could do better, the job of writing the banners would be his.

Footy banners are a unique tradition in Australian sport which dates back to the 1930s. The huge banners were originally made from crepe paper and suspended on tall poles held by members of the club cheer squad so that players could run through them on their entry to the field while the club song plays. A message is always displayed on the banner and the message that exasperated McGinlay that day was: *We are here to do our best so victory will be ours*. Could the words have been more wishy-washy? Could the phrasing have been more flat?

McGinlay set about trying to inject a little attitude and humour. The next week, with the Bulldogs playing away to Port Adelaide in Adelaide, his banner read:

WESTERN BULLDOGS
UNDEFEATED AT ADELAIDE OVAL
BE AFRAID
PORT ADELAIDE

This was funny because the Bulldogs had never played at the Adelaide Oval, as it had only become Port Adelaide's home ground that season. So of course the Bulldogs were undefeated there!

By 2016, McGinlay had well and truly found his groove. In Round 15 at the SCG against the

Sydney Swans, his banner had a hilarious crack at Sydney's lockout laws, which mandated the early closing of pubs and bars in response to a spate of alcohol-fuelled violence on the streets:

WE'LL WIN THIS GAME
AND PARTY TILL LATE
OR AT LEAST TILL ALL
YOUR PUBS CLOSE AT 8

Later that season, the Bulldogs faced the GWS Giants in the preliminary final, again in Sydney. This time, McGinlay took a swipe at the fact that the Giants had been invented as a bit of a thought bubble by the AFL in a region where Australian rules footy is largely a foreign culture:

OUR CLUB WAS BORN
IN BLOOD AND BOOTS
NOT IN
AFL FOCUS GROUPS

Ouch!

The Bulldogs won that game, thus making the grand final – a remarkable feat for a team that had finished seventh in the regular season. They went on to win the flag too, becoming the first premiership team from outside the top four since the current top-eight finals system was adopted in 2000.

Naturally, people were expecting big things from his banner on grand final day. Many expressed disappointment that it wasn't roll-in-the-aisles funny, but I always thought it was poignant and hit the right note. Switching the letters in the last word to turn Bulldogs into

Bullgods (and rhyme with odds) was a subtle but brilliant touch.

WE'VE BEATEN
ALL THE OTHERS
DEFIED ALL OF THE ODDS
TODAY THIS TEAM
OF PUPPIES
BECOME THE BULLGODS

McGinlay no longer does the Bulldogs banners, but his legacy lives on, with a generally more humorous tone to many banners these days. Not that there weren't many other great ones down the years.

In 2021, former GWS banner writer Matthew Hagias and former GWS head of media and communications Leigh Meyrick wrote a book which surely had one of the cleverest titles in Australian publishing history. It was called *Footy Banners: A Complete Run-Through,* as in, you run through the banners and they're running through the best ones. Did you really need that explained? You didn't, did you? And that's precisely the point about footy banners. Whether they contain in-jokes or heartfelt messages, they need no explanation. They are the language of sport writ large enough for fans in the highest row of the Shane Warne Stand at The 'G to read, and they are part of what makes the language of Australian sport so rich.

Spectacular Aussie sporting names: *Ned Zelic*

In the beginning, the surnames of our Socceroos were all Anglo. Way back in 1922, the first three Socceroos had the surnames

Gibb, Cartwright and Cumberford, which sounds like a London law firm. It took until the 1970s for Slavic, Greek and Italian names to start appearing on the list of national reps. Today, there are increasing numbers of African names on the list of players to have donned the green and gold.

The eighties and nineties were a golden period for Socceroo names when many players had a combination of an Anglo first name and a non-Anglo surname. These sons of migrants sometimes had first names that were Anglicised versions of their given names like Ned (given name Nedjeljko) Zelic, Eddie (given name Eduvard) Krncevic and Paul (given name Paolo) Trimboli. More commonly, the Anglicised first names were the players' actual given names, like Charlie Yankos, Frank Farina, Stan Lazaridis, Jason and Michael Petkovic and

AT SIXES AND SEVENS

This saying is not unique to Australian sport but is used widely here to describe a team whose formation has lost all shape in attack or defence. It is especially common in rugby league with its (usually) orderly attacking and defensive lines. The origins of the phrase are said to date back to an early dice game which was a little like modern day craps, in which the numbers five and six were the most dangerous numbers to shoot for, so if you did, you were in all sorts of mental disarray. Somehow five and six ended up as six and seven. The phrase first appeared in print in English author Geoffrey Chaucer's epic poem *Troilus and Criseyde*, which contains the couplet:

> 'But manly sette the world on sixe and sevene;
> And, if thou deye a martir, go to hevene.'

This is getting seriously spooky here, because as you can see, Chaucer's poem from the 1380s actually contains the name of a rugby league team: Manly! And now the phrase from that very line is widely used in rugby league. Where's the *Twilight Zone* music when you need it?

John Aloisi, who famously scored the penalty against Uruguay in Sydney that put Australia into the 2006 FIFA World Cup, and who is also the only Australian to have played in Europe's three most prestigious leagues: Italy's Serie A, Spain's La Liga and the UK's Premier League.

Aloisi was always a personal favourite player. His goal against Japan in the 2006 FIFA World Cup was pure artistry and poise. As a kid I also loved Charlie Yankos, who captained the Socceroos thirty times between 1986 and 1989. Yankos scored an amazing goal from a wickedly swirling free kick against Argentina in the 1998 Bicentennial Gold Cup, a friendly tournament which featured Australia, Argentina, Brazil and Saudi Arabia. For the record, Australia finished runner-up to Brazil after beating Argentina 4–1 thanks in part to that Yankos thunderbolt.

In terms of names, my favourite was always Ned Zelic. Any first or last name starting with Z is always cool, and even though the name Ned Zelic isn't quite as spectacular as that of French superstar Zinedine Zidane (because no one's name is), I always loved the way Ned Zelic sounded a little like a modern Australian multicultural version of 'Ned Kelly'.

As for the actual title of the men's national team, it is ironic that a team with the word 'soccer' in it falls under the auspices of a governing body now known as Football Australia. You can see how it happened. The body was originally called the Australian Soccer Federation when established in 1961, to differentiate itself from other football codes. Then the culture changed and football in Australia decided to get with the rest of the world, give or take the USA and Canada, both of which still staunchly call the game 'soccer'. You have to wonder whether the Socceroos would be called the 'Footballroos' if they started from scratch in Australia today.

Great Aussie sporting terms: *Go you good thing!*

This is one of those phrases that is pure joy to say or, more likely, shout. It was popularised by former Wallabies prop turned rugby colour commentator Chris 'Buddha' Handy. In passionate, often quavering tones, he would shout, 'Go you good thing' as a player crossed for a try. The phrase has become an Australian rugby staple used by commentators and fans alike.

Chris Handy's catchcry has become a very handy weapon in the barracking arsenal in other sports too. The phrase 'Go you good thing' briefly travelled nationwide at the end of the Sydney 2000 Olympics with a song of that name sung by John Farnham at the end of Roy and HG's final episode of their cult TV show *The Dream*. But it's still not widely used outside Queensland and New South Wales, where fans bellow it out at a variety of sports, including horse racing, where they already had the phrase 'good thing' to mean a horse that is considered almost certain to win. This, of course, means it almost certainly won't.

Great Aussie sporting terms: *Minor premiership*

Win the grand final and you win the premiership. Finish top of the ladder before the finals and you win the minor premiership. No other nation uses this term.

You get actual silverware for being minor premiers. In the NRL, the prize is the JJ Giltinan

Shield, the trophy that used to be awarded to the premiers up until 1981. For the premiers, the shield was replaced by the iconic Provan–Summons trophy, a three-dimensional cast of a famous 1963 photograph, 'The Gladiators', which featured mud-caked players Norm Provan and Arthur Summons after the 1963 grand final between St George and Western Suburbs – which St George won, the eighth in their remarkable streak of eleven consecutive premierships.

The term 'minor premiership' is used in several sports, including the A-League, which has a finals series, unlike the major European football leagues. And while nobody is too excited about being minor premiers in real time because the finals lie ahead and it's all about winning the grand final, it's always nice to have an extra ornament to display in the trophy cabinet at the footy club.

The term originates from an old Aussie rules footy tradition, where games in the regular season were referred to as 'minor rounds', and finals were called 'major rounds'.

Interestingly, between the years 2000 and 2023, in both the NRL and AFL, only nine of the twenty-four minor premiers went on to win the grand final.

Great Aussie sporting terms: *Maggot*

We live in enlightened times, but occasionally, you can't help feeling they're a little too enlightened. Booing the umpire or referee in any sport is undoubtedly rude – they're just doing their job after all and, like any of us, are human and therefore prone to error. The thing is, booing the match officials is part of the experience of attending live professional sport. This is obviously not the case in community or junior sport, but when you've paid a hefty price to sit in a windswept seat in the outer at professional sport, you kind of feel like the price of admission includes the right to vent at dud decisions.

Fortunately, Aussie rules footy fans have the perfect solution. They use the word 'maggot', a reference to the days when the umps wore all-white uniforms rather than the fluoro colours they usually now wear. Seen from afar, they really did look like little white maggots, so today, when you scream 'MAGGOT' in rasping tones because you didn't like the free kick that the idiot with the whistle awarded to the other team, tell anyone who objects that you are merely engaging in visual verisimilitude and, if they ask you what the hell that means, tell them to google it and hope they don't call your bluff.

Spectacular Aussie sporting names: *Fuifui Moimoi*

A beautiful thing has happened in NRL commentary in recent seasons: commentators have started to pronounce Pasifika names properly. Take, for example, Josh Papali'i the veteran Canberra Raiders forward who has also represented Queensland in State of Origin and both Australia and Samoa in international rugby league. They used to say it like 'pa-pah-lee'. But somewhere along the line, word got around that accent was being placed on the wrong syllables, and that two vowels separated by an apostrophe constituted two distinct syllables. So now even

PAPER-THIN DEFENCE

Hooray. Your team just got smashed by a million points again. Someone really ought to do something about that defensive setup which is so weak, your players might as well be origami figures.

the biggest boofhead in the box enunciates it 'papa-lee-ee' and the world is a more accurate, respectful and beautiful place.

Another example is champion Penrith winger Brian To'o, which everyone pronounces correctly as 'Toh-oh'.

Long prominent in all sports in New Zealand, especially the rugby codes, players of Pacific Islands heritage took much longer to break into the rugby codes in large numbers here in Australia. Partly, that was demographics. The number of Australians with Pasifika ancestry almost doubled from 178,000 to 337,000 in the fifteen years between the 2006 and 2021 censuses. This was more or less the period during which their presence in the rugby codes swelled massively. Take a look at the NRL grand final line-ups of those two census years and you can see the wave of migration reflected. In the 2006 NRL Grand Final, there were just two Pacific Islander names among the thirty-four starting players and reserves. In the 2021 decider, there were at least ten in total. Indeed, as many as forty-five per cent of NRL players now identify as being of Pacific Islands or Māori heritage.

There have been too many good players of Pasifika heritage to name in recent years, but one that all fans loved was Fuifui Moimoi, the 201-game Parramatta Eels enforcer. 'Moimoi was known for his cannonball charges, his unpredictable and rapidly changing hairstyles, being a man of few words and arguably the best alliterative name ever to grace a rugby league field,' the NRL's official website wrote in 2015. Hard to disagree – except for the bit about alliteration, which technically means consecutive words that start with the same sound, not repeated sounds within words. Looks like the NRL's error-prone referees have been writing the website copy in the off-season.

Great Aussie sporting terms: *Drongo*

Calling someone a 'drongo' is a delightfully old-fashioned Aussie putdown for someone who's a little hapless or dopey. While it's not a phrase used specifically in a sporting context – or used much anywhere anymore – it's included here because it has sporting origins.

A drongo is a species of bird, but it was also an Australian racehorse of the 1920s that raced thirty-seven times without winning. Poor old Drongo wasn't as bad as all that. He finished runner-up five times and third on seven occasions, and one of those second-placed finishes was in the time-honoured Victoria Derby. He also finished fourth in the Adelaide Cup. Drongo's problem was that he was well-bred and raced in the highest company, but always fell short of expectations. There were, are and always will be countless much slower, plodding horses going round each week in bush races, but life is unfair – horse racing doubly so – and Drongo has thus been immortalised.

Great Aussie sporting terms: *Claret*

'Claret' is blood and it's pronounced so it rhymes with 'carrot'. When a player is accidentally cut, any commentator over the age of about forty will inevitably go, 'Ooooh, there's plenty of claret coming out of that nasty gash.'

But why claret? The term dates itself to the mid-twentieth century, when claret was a favoured varietal of red wine. Claret could occasionally be the good stuff, but mostly it was the cheap junk they put in cask wine in the 1970s. These days, you rarely see claret in bottle shops in Australia because European authorities dictated that the term could only be used for wine made in the Bordeaux region of France. But claret is still common parlance in Australian sport, perhaps because an injured player oozing 'cabernet sauvignon' just doesn't have the same to ring to it.

On the subject of forbidden booze names, it's worth mentioning that the same thing happened to champagne. Once upon a time, you could ferment your own white wine grapes, carbonate it, bottle it and call it champers. Not anymore. Now it has to come from the Champagne wine region. Fortunately, that hasn't stopped us referring to a particularly skilful or exciting passage of play as 'champagne football'. 'Sparkling white wine football' doesn't quite have the same ring to it.

Great Aussie sporting terms: *Falcon*

A falcon, or the act of being 'falconed', is when you're hit on the head with the ball. It applies to a variety of Australian sports. The falcon has even taken wings and is starting to be used overseas.

Why a falcon?

It all goes back to Mario Fenech, the Maltese-born Australian rugby league player, known as 'The Maltese Falcon' after the famous movie, who notched up 274 games for South Sydney, North Sydney and the short-lived

EXCITEMENT MACHINE

Players who don't just excel at their chosen sport but who bring a little bit of X factor are often described by commentators as an 'excitement machine'. When you think about it, it sounds a little like an amusement park ride, a little like something you might purchase at an adult store, and a little like the polar opposite of Marvin, the perennially depressed android from *The Hitchhiker's Guide to the Galaxy*.

expansion team, the South Queensland Crushers. In 1995, Fenech was limping off the field injured while playing for the Crushers when his teammate Ray Herring unwittingly passed a ball that went – klonk! – right into Mario's head. It was, it must be said, a very South Queensland Crushers piece of play. In their three seasons of existence at the top level, they won two wooden spoons and finished sixteenth the other year.

As for the original falcon incident, Fenech was a member of the panel on Channel 9's *The Footy Show* at the time and when the producer suggested including the footage for a laugh, Fenech was unamused and insisted the footage be consigned to the cutting room floor. But present-day Brisbane Broncos coach Kevin Walters was also on the panel and convinced the producer to run it, unbeknownst to Fenech. When it aired, Fenech was furious. They say there were harsh words and headlocks in the ad break. But the comical moment struck a chord with fans and from then on, any ball contact with the head was called a falcon.

There are two little add-ons to the tale, one funny, the other poignant. The funny one is that rugby league commentator Andrew Voss took it upon himself to contact the thrower of the original falcon pass, Ray Herring, for a segment on a show. 'I've been waiting twenty years for someone to call me!' Herring told him.

The poignant ending is that Mario Fenech was diagnosed with early onset dementia at the age of fifty-three. Doctors say he has chronic traumatic encephalopathy, better known as CTE. Fenech and his family have been open about his condition, hoping to raise awareness of the long-term repercussions of head injuries. It is a sad irony that a man who suffered so many serious head knocks is now synonymous with being struck in the head in a benign way.

Spectacular Aussie sporting names: *Che Cockatoo-Collins*

Take an Argentine rebel who became a Cuban revolutionary, mix it with a raspy-voiced cheeky Australian bird, add a sober Anglo name that is a type of dictionary, stir, put in the oven for twenty minutes at 180 degrees, and you've got yourself the most beautiful name.

A 200-gamer in the AFL, Cockatoo-Collins was sadly delisted a year short of Port Adelaide's only premiership to date (2004) but worse things happen in life than failing to attain sporting glory. He has since become a respected voice in Indigenous affairs within the business and political spheres.

Great Aussie sporting terms: *Carn!*

Some Australian slang is almost impossible to explain to foreigners. You can expect a puzzled face when you tell them that 'sarvo' means 'this arvo', as in 'this afternoon', or that 'Straya' means 'Australia'. Why do we abbreviate words in this manner? Why are we so busy, or perhaps so lazy, that the letter 'l' in our country's name is sacrificed?

Whatever the reason, the great Aussie sporting word 'carn' is in the category where a consonant is sacrificed. Quite simply it means 'come on' as in 'Come on, you Blues!' Or as the fans say, 'Caaaaaaarn, you Blues!'

As a side note, tennis star Lleyton Hewitt

popularised the phrase 'Come on!' in a stellar career that took him to world number one, the 2001 US Open title and 2002 Wimbledon crown. Hewitt would yell, 'Come oooooon!' after almost every winning point but since his retirement, few Aussie sport fans have bellowed the phrase as two distinct words. When you're seated in row ZZ in the nosebleeds of The 'G and the winter southerly is howling and you've got a mouthful of lukewarm Four'N Twenty, it's much easier to let rip with one drawn-out syllable.

Great Aussie sporting terms: *Worm burner*

Australians have many fantastic words for kicks. A torpedo kick is a term used worldwide for a kick where the ball spins about its long axis like a torpedo, enabling it to travel maximum distance. But only Australians abbreviate it to 'torp'. In Aussie rules footy, when you put a bit of grunt into a kick, you are said to be giving it a 'roost'. And if the kick doesn't come off the boot so well, it's a 'mongrel punt'. Rugby league has the 'grubber', an attacking kick which dribbles along the ground and is difficult to defend because of the unpredictability of the bounce. This term is surely a very close cousin of cricket's 'mullygrubber'. You can even say that a kick is 'grubbering', because the second rule of Australian linguistic life after 'everything must be abbreviated' is 'any noun can become a verb'.

But surely the greatest Australian word for any type of kick is a 'worm burner'. There's a suggestion that 'grubber' has something to do with the grubs that live in the ground, but there's absolutely no doubt that a worm

TAKE THE GAME BY THE SCRUFF OF THE NECK

The game is not going well. The game is not where you want it to be. Thus do you switch to mother cat mode and metaphorically pick the game up by the scruff of the neck and carry the game to where you want it to be. Only the true greats of any game have the capacity to take control of proceedings in this manner.

burner is speaking directly about subterranean invertebrates. Most worm burners are accidental, but occasionally a deliberate worm burner is kicked for strategic purposes. Sometimes a worm burner is called a 'daisy cutter', a term which is also quite common for a mis-hit low driver or iron shot in golf.

For those who love grammar, worm burner is a classic example of assonance, which is when the vowels of different words sound the same but the end consonant is different so it can't technically be classed as a rhyme. Who says you learn nothing reading sports books?

Great Aussie sporting quirks: *Commentary box brilliance*

'And he's done it.'

For more than thirty years, I have pondered the deeper meaning of this phrase.

In 1993, a 23-year-old Shane Warne bowled what is now known as the Ball of the Century, or simply The Gatting Ball, to accomplished English batter Mike Gatting. We've all seen the video. A young, bleached-blond Warney approaches the crease at Old Trafford in Manchester for his first ball of Test cricket in England. The ball leaves his hand, drifts and dips toward the leg side, pitches well outside leg stump before turning viciously the other way and crashing into the off stump. Gatting doesn't know what has happened. The portly stalwart of the English batting order stands there, literally not understanding the source of the commotion as jubilant Aussie fielders race to embrace Warne. How could a ball start over THERE and end up THERE? Or, as the late English sports journalist Martin Johnson cheekily wrote that evening: 'How anyone can spin a ball the width of Gatting boggles the mind.'

Meanwhile, in the commentary box, the late great Richie Benaud simply said, 'And he's done it.' This, when you think about it, was a very unusual piece of commentary. Done what exactly? You'd normally break out a phrase like that when you've done a specific thing you set out to achieve. Let's say, for example, it was the closing stages of a match and Australia needed one wicket to win and the captain handed the ball to Warne. He takes the wicket and the commentator says, 'And he's done it.' This would make sense. But England were 1 for 80 on day two of a five-day Test with the match evenly poised and still very much in its formative stages. So what exactly did Benaud mean? What exactly had Warne 'done'?

In deconstructing this comment from the doyen of cricket commentators, I thought it might be fun to ask the doyen of cricket writers, Melbourne-based Gideon Haigh, what he made of it.

'It's a nice bit of commentary, but I'm not sure Benaud meant much at all. You can speculate too deeply on these things,' Haigh responded.

With enormous respect to Gideon, who knows infinitely more about such things than me, my gut response to his comment was in line with another great Australian sporting phrase, 'Yeah, nah', leaning heavily toward 'nah'.

My feeling has always been that Benaud was speaking of something much deeper than the ball he had witnessed. Benaud had of course been a leg spinner himself. There had been Australian leg spinners since him, but they had usually been fringe members of the team – valuable contributors at times but rarely the stars. But here was Warne, making leg spin pure rock 'n' roll. And that's what I believe Benaud was hinting at, possibly without realising it himself. Warne, in one ball, had breathed new life into the thing that Benaud considered most beautiful in cricket, but feared was a lost art in his home country. Here was a young leg spinner bowling what to this day is regarded as the greatest ball ever bowled.

Benaud passed away in 2015 and will forever be missed. His commentary was dry and famously understated to the point of being minimalist, but there was logic behind that approach. Benaud always said you should never tell a television viewer what they could see for themselves. Today's cricket commentators would do well to heed that lesson.

Admittedly, cricket itself has changed with the advent of Twenty20, so the hype factor has been turbocharged, but there are guys in the commentary box who get as excited as lottery winners when someone hits a regulation six – or a 'maximum' as they now call it – in an early season midweek Big Bash match, when the kids are still in school and there are more seagulls than spectators.

Without doubt, Benaud holds the mantle of the greatest Australian sporting commentator of all time in any sport. If you want to see him at his best, type 'Benaud underarm' into the YouTube search bar. There you will find a man who rarely editorialised rightly condemn Australia's lowest sporting moment, the day Trevor Chappell bowled an underarm ball to prevent New Zealand batter Brian McKechnie being able to hit a match-winning six off the last ball of the game, under orders from his skipper and brother Greg.

'Let me just tell you what I think about it. I think it was a disgraceful performance from a captain who got his sums wrong today, and I think it should never be permitted to happen again. We keep reading and hearing that the players are under a lot of pressure and that they're tired and jaded – perhaps their judgement and their skill is blunted – well, perhaps they might advance that as an excuse for what happened out there today. Not with me they don't. I think it was a very poor performance, one of the worst things I have ever seen done on a cricket field. Good night.'

Richie truly was a man of the people. But naturally, we have had plenty of other great commentators down the years. All passionate sporting nations have produced great commentators and it would be indefensibly boastful to say that ours are better than theirs. But it's still worth celebrating some of the great Australian commentary moments and personalities of recent times.

The late great Norman May delivered the country's most famous call at the Olympics in the final of the men's 4 x 100m swimming medley relay final at the Moscow 1980 Olympics, when Neil Brooks edged out the Soviet champion Sergey Koplyakov in front of the latter's adoring home fans. Interestingly, his call has been misquoted over the years. Most people think it was 'Gold, gold, gold for Australia' and that's become a phrase that people still use in the context of anything in Australian life being desirable or excellent. In fact, May said, 'Gold! Gold to Australia.

Gold!' But it was still a great call. While it might not look like much on the page, look it up and give it a listen. I promise you'll feel differently.

Sometimes a commentator's job is to display unwavering neutrality. At the Olympics, that is rarely the case.

Cathy Freeman winning the 400m at the Sydney Olympics tops most people's list of the greatest Australian Olympic moments, but the commentary was the perfect accompaniment. After Freeman crossed the line, Bruce McAvaney simply said, 'What a legend, what a champion.' Then there was silence for a good twenty seconds before co-commentator Raelene Boyle made it the perfect trio by adding, 'What a relief.' And when you looked at Freeman's face, you could see that was exactly what she was feeling.

McAvaney is one of our greats. Some also find him a little grating. His tone is sometimes a little too syrupy when his emotions rise to the surface ... which is most of the time. That said, none can deny his passion or knowledge across virtually all sports, especially his great loves of AFL, athletics and horse racing. And syrupy works when the person beside you in the box is dry, which is why it was always so enjoyable listening to Bruce McAvaney commentating the AFL footy alongside Dennis Cometti.

Cometti was the best and confetti are the rest. End of argument. He will always be remembered for saying some of the cleverest off-the-cuff lines ever uttered by anyone, anywhere. When Western Bulldogs champion Tony Liberatore entered a pack of players and got poked in the eye, Cometti said, 'He went in optimistically, but came out misty optically.' Whose brain works that fast?

Another great Aussie rules footy duo was Peter Landy and Lou Richards. Landy was the straight caller, even if his jackets were on the garish side. If you ever thought Ron Burgundy's outfit was ridiculously outlandish in the movie *Anchorman* (because come on, no one actually ever presented news in a burgundy jacket), then you never saw Peter Landy on a Saturday afternoon back in the late 1970s and early eighties. Clothing aside, further colour in the commentary box was added by old 'Louie the Lip', who would chime in with trademark phrases like 'wobbly old punt kick' and nicknames that he coined for players like 'The Flying Doormat' for rock-solid Carlton defender Bruce Doull, who sported a trailing mat of hair behind his heavily balding head.

Around the same time, Rex Mossop was king of the rugby league commentary box. My dad always used to call him 'Rex Messup' as he had a talent for butchering the language and littering his commentary with malapropisms – words or phrases that he got slightly wrong. A classic Australian sporting malapropism is a player saying 'it all goes well for the future' when they mean 'it augurs well'. Not sure if Rex ever delivered that one but I do recall a wardrobe full of fur-lined jackets and red skivvies. Commentary fashion was just as entertaining as the footy back in the day.

The greatest rugby league caller of modern times was indisputably Ray Warren. Much of his appeal lay in his voice, but there was more to it than that. My wife once passed by the TV and said, 'That man sounds polite,' and there was indeed something delightfully old-fashioned in Ray's manner and delivery. Warren honed his commentary craft on racecourses, where race callers are taught to have sympathy for the favourites, which the majority of punters have backed. Perhaps because of his background, there was always empathy in his tone. Without cheering one way or the other, Ray saw what we saw and Ray felt what we felt. 'That's not a try, that's a miracle!' was his memorable call as Queensland's Mark Coyne planted the ball over the line in the seventy-ninth minute of Game I of the 1994 State of Origin series for a near length-of-the-field try that sealed a famous comeback victory.

If one type of Australian sports commentator sits clearly atop the world, it would have to be race callers. American race callers do something that is unthinkable to Australians: they call only the first few runners. In Australia, callers do a run-through of the field so that even if you've backed a three-legged donkey which is half a lap behind the field, the caller will at least have the courtesy of informing you. This is an interesting cultural difference and speaks to Australian egalitarianism versus America's obsession with winners.

That's what the best commentators do in any sport. They make you feel like it matters as much to them as it does to you. So, really, it doesn't matter what Richie Benaud meant by 'and he's done it'. The brief phrase likely meant something different to every one of the millions of viewers who watched the ball in real time or in replays. Yet it captured the emotion that each of us felt and that, ultimately, is a commentator's first and last job.

Spectacular Aussie sporting names: *Aliir Aliir*

There are plenty of good players of African heritage coming into the AFL these days, but Aliir Aliir is so good, they named him twice!

Born to South Sudanese parents in a Kenyan refugee camp, Aliir's family moved to Australia when the boy was eight, settling in Brisbane. A tick over twenty years later, the classy defender has racked up more than 150 games in total for Port Adelaide and his former team the Sydney Swans, and was named in the 2021 All Australian team.

Great Aussie sporting terms: *The 'G*

One letter. That's all it takes to send chills down a nation's spine. That letter is of course the letter g as in 'The 'G' which of course means the MCG, which of course means the Melbourne Cricket Ground, which many consider the beating heart of Australian sport. Abbreviating an acronym is just about the most Australian thing you can do.

Great Aussie sporting terms: *Ping*

'Ping' actually means two different things in Australian rules footy. It can mean an attempted shot at goal or, more commonly, it is used in the past tense to mean a player has been penalised by the umpire, with a free kick awarded to the opposition. The term 'pinged' is not used ubiquitously in other sports but it has definitely travelled north of the Murray River. You'll occasionally even hear it in everyday language. For example, if you get a speeding ticket, you can say you were pinged by the cops.

Ping appears in one other context relating to Aussie rules footy. You don't hear it much anymore, but detractors used to call it 'aerial ping-pong'.

Funny story about ping-pong. Working for a sports magazine back in 2008, I wrote a preview for the Aussie team at the Beijing Olympics, with a brief interview with one athlete in each sport. I can't remember the name of the table tennis athlete, but he had flaming red hair and our brilliant British subeditor gave the story the genius headline 'The ginga pinga', as in a ginger-haired person who plays ping-pong (the term 'pinga' bore no reference to 'pingers', an Aussie slang word for ecstasy pills). Anyway, the magazine hit the newsstands and the athlete's dad called. It's always nice when people are happy and take the time to tell you.

PREMIERSHIP DROUGHT

When South Sydney won the NRL premiership in 2014, it broke a premiership drought going back to 1971. When the Sydney Swans won the 2005 AFL flag, it broke a 72-year premiership drought dating all the way back to 1933 (when the Swans were called South Melbourne). 'Premiership drought' is a classic Aussie saying for a lengthy gap between titles, and in this driest continent on earth, who doesn't imagine players out there on a parched, cracked surface when they hear the phrase?

'Great story about my son, Anthony. Table tennis gets so little publicity, we really appreciate it.'

'My pleasure.'

'Just one question.'

'Sure.'

'What's a ginga pinga?'

'Ummm ... so you know how your son's got red hair? Well, you see ...'

Spectacular Aussie sporting names: *Bradman Best*

He plays in the centres for the Newcastle Knights in the NRL, he has worn the blue jersey of New South Wales in State of Origin with great distinction, shrugging off two defenders to score the crucial try that set NSW on track to win the Origin series decider in Brisbane in 2024, and he was born with the surname Best. So naturally his parents gave him a fitting first name to go along with it.

Great Aussie sporting quirks:
Our obsession with comedy

Almost a quarter of a century after the Sydney 2000 Olympics, Australians who are old enough to have watched it will remember a few key moments. There was Sydney schoolgirl Nikki Webster flying through the air on barely visible wires at the Opening Ceremony.

There was Cathy Freeman, all poise and grace as she lit the Olympic flame despite a brief equipment malfunction, and no less ice-veined as she stormed to victory in the 400m.

There was Ian Thorpe and friends winning a bunch of stuff in the pool.

And there was Rampaging Roy Slaven and HG Nelson.

Roy and HG's show *The Dream*, which came on Channel 7 at the end of each long day of Olympic action, was initially planned as a televisual nightcap. But the sideshow soon became as big as the main event and delivered some of the best entertainment of the Games.

Athletes of the world discovered it and became hooked. Whether it was the hilarious commentary at the gymnastics with terms like 'hello boys!', the 'crazy date' and the 'battered sav', or Roy's comical commentary on the table tennis which simply went 'ping, pong, ping, pong, ping, pong ...' Roy and HG turned the world's biggest sporting event into a massive laugh-fest and the whole world loved it.

'If it wasn't for this show, I'd probably be the gold medallist, because I sat up so many nights and watched this and laughed,' American sprinter Jon Drummond told Roy and HG on the final night of the show. 'It's your fault!'

Drummond had finished fifth in the 100m final behind compatriot Maurice Greene, and realistically was never going to beat Greene, even though he was good enough to win gold as part of the 4 x 100m relay. But he made a great point: Roy and HG were unmissable. You might have the most important event of your life tomorrow, but you'd still sit up and watch them. Roy and HG were – and you really have to say it – comedy gold.

Sport and comedy are inseparable in Australian life. When other countries combine sport and comedy, there is often a respectful buffer between the two, a safe zone so no one is cutting too close to the bone. Adam Sandler's classic 1996 golf spoof *Happy Gilmore* was wildly slapstick and completely removed from reality. But we do sport and comedy in real time, taking the piss not only out of the funny stuff in sport, but out of ourselves and our own obsessions.

There are, and have been, too many comedic Australian sports shows on TV and radio over the years to list. There have also been too many funny people in sport, like rugby's Nick Cummins (aka the 'Honey Badger') and cricket's Kerry O'Keeffe and rugby league's Matty Johns and countless characters in Aussie rules footy down the years.

There have also been individuals who never played the game but satirised the hell out of it. Billy Birmingham is perhaps the most successful. Through his Twelfth Man persona, he turned an iconic era of cricket and cricket commentary into comedy gold. Who'll ever forget his assessment of Richie Benaud's penchant for light-coloured jackets, describing his options as cream, bone, white, off-white, ivory or beige. You wouldn't call Birmingham's humour vanilla, that's for sure! More recently, *The Grade Cricketer* podcast has brilliantly satirised the aspirations of every bog-ordinary suburban or bush cricketer who ever pulled on a pair of pads.

Denis Carnahan is a musician, sound engineer, staunch Canberra Raiders fan and the one-man act behind *Cricket the Musical* and *Rugby League the Musical*. About ten years ago, he wrote a song that went viral on YouTube called 'That's in Queensland'. The song parodied the fact that in the State of Origin series, Queensland was cynically interpreting the rules to include players whose origins were definitely not in Queensland: 'Where is Sydney? That's in Queensland!'

That, right there, is the very essence of Australian comedy. Take something that kind of inherently sucks, that everyone can see is plain wrong, but don't get angry at it. Don't whinge or whine. Take the piss. Have a laugh. Because while sport is one of the most important things to Australians, that doesn't stop us from seeing the funny side. And that might just be the healthiest thing about our sporting culture.

Spectacular Aussie sporting names: *Héritier Lumumba*

You could literally write an entire book on the great names of Aussie rules footy. We could have done separate entries for Orazio Fantasia, Robert DiPierdomenico and countless others. But Héritier Lumumba is a name that is both colourful and pivotal in the context of our acceptance of unusual names.

Instrumental in Collingwood's 2010 premiership, he was then known as Harry O'Brien. This was because his surname was changed when he was nine years old, and he was given the nickname Harry. But by 2013, Lumumba was proudly playing under his full birth name as he sought to celebrate his identity as an Australian of Brazilian and mixed-African descent.

Lumumba had a well-publicised falling out with Collingwood, alleging he was the victim of numerous racist nicknames. In 2021, Collingwood released a report called *Do Better*, an independent review that challenged the club to confront racism. Lumumba's allegations were not directly addressed in the report, but everyone knew they underpinned its very existence.

Australia has thankfully started to move on and grow up. A player born Héritier Lumumba would surely now stay that way, their ethnic heritage embraced by fans and teammates alike.

Great Aussie sporting terms: *Grand final*

Most major sporting competitions around the world have a final. Tennis majors have finals. The FIFA World Cup has a final. But Australians call the final match of the season in our major domestic sporting competitions the grand final. Why?

Writer and sports historian Sean Fagan touched on the topic back in the 2000s on the website he used to run called *RL1908*, its name a reference to the year 1908, when the first New South Wales Rugby League competition took place and, for the record, was won by the South Sydney Rabbitohs. In an article simply titled 'The Grand Final', Fagan explained that, in

FIGHT TOOTH AND NAIL

There's nothing mysterious about the origins of the phrase 'to fight tooth and nail', which simply means to use any resources at your disposal to get the job done. But it's pretty funny to see it taken literally with a tooth and a nail slugging it out in the ring. So who would win? Naily looks sharp and would surely chip away at Toothy's enamel. But old Toothy might do a Mike Tyson and bite Naily's ear off. Actually, Naily has no ears. Looks like Toothy will just have to bite his head off then.

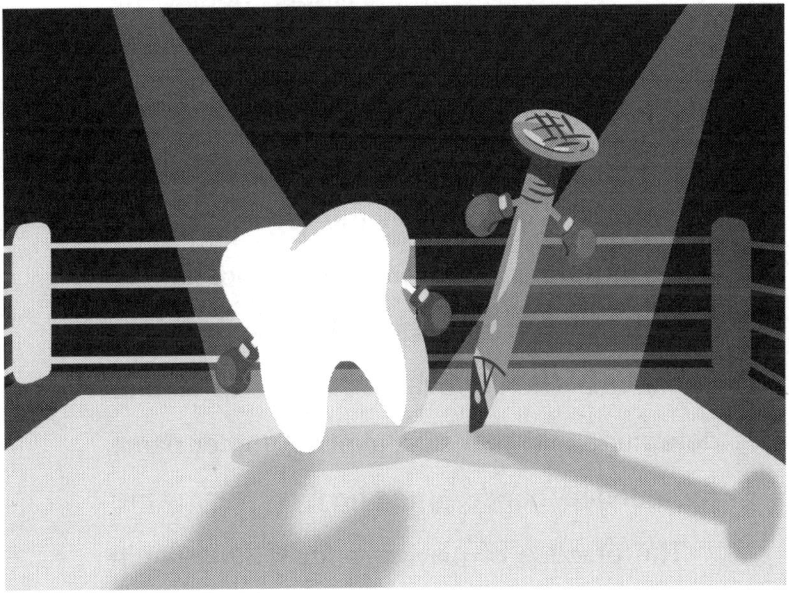

the old days, the NSWRL premiers were usually decided by whichever team finished top. In this respect, it was like the English Premier League and most other contemporary global football leagues (but not Australia's A-League, which also has a grand final).

There was an exception to the old NSWRL rule of the top team on the ladder winning the whole shebang. If the top two teams finished within two points (one win) of each other on the ladder, a final would be played. Points were up for grabs, just like in the regular season, so if the second-placed team happened to win, the two teams would then be equal on the ladder. Then you'd have a second final to determine that year's premiers. Another name was needed, hence: grand final.

The practice of playing a finals series each season with one mandatory match that decided the season's champions only came into vogue in 1931 in the VFL and 1954 in the NSWRL. In both codes, it was known as the grand final.

Calling the deciding match of the season the grand final is not our only quirk of terminology around end-of-season matches. Australians, it must be said, have a strange relationship with the word 'semi-final'.

As any fan knows, a semi-final in most sports is the qualifying match for the final. Tennis is a great example. Everyone knows that the semis are one step short of the final. It's a similar story with knockout competitions in a range of sports. But we Aussies have mangled the word semi-finals two ways.

First, we used to call the whole finals series leading up to the grand final the 'semi-finals' or sometimes, 'the semis'. You rarely hear this anymore, but it was once extremely common, especially in rugby league, to hear players talking about their team's aim being to make 'the semis', meaning the finals series.

The other weird thing we do is calling the wrong match a semi-final. Here's how that goes. The finals series in both the AFL and NRL takes place over four weeks. The elimination finals are in week one. The semi-finals are in week two. The preliminary finals are in week three. Week four is the grand final. See the problem? The matches we call semi-finals are technically a week early.

For example, in the 2017 NRL season, the Parramatta Eels were knocked out by the North Queensland Cowboys in the semi-finals. Most people on planet Earth would take that to mean they fell one match short of the grand final. Nope! Their losing semi-final was the week before that.

Why pick that particular example? Because the Eels' leading try-scorer that year was the flying Fijian winger Semi Radradra (who, for the record, went on to win an Olympic gold medal for Fiji in Rugby Sevens at the Tokyo 2020 Olympics). It's kind of ironic that Semi lost a semi that wasn't actually a semi.

Great Aussie sporting terms: *Wooden spoon*

In sport, winning is always the goal. Or is it?

In Australian sport, the prize for coming last in team sports competitions is the wooden spoon, which no one wants to win. Actually, that's not technically true because the wooden spooner in the AFL gets the first pick of fresh talent in the draft at the end of the season. So when two teams are both teetering on the brink, let's just say they don't have enormous incentive to find a late-season burst of form.

The term wooden spoon is an Australian classic. It appears here and there around the world, but nowhere else is it a ubiquitous part of the language. It's also not relevant in many overseas sporting leagues. They don't use it in European football because of the relegation and promotion system, and American sports competitions are generally broken into leagues, divisions and/or conferences, so there is no single table for all teams, and therefore no official last-placed team.

But Australia has the wooden spoon, or sometimes just 'the spoon'. Fortunately, there is no trophy, otherwise the trophy cabinets at teams like the AFL's North Melbourne Kangaroos, the NRL's Wests Tigers and the BBL's Sydney Thunder would be adorned with a lot of timber cutlery.

Teams are said to 'win' the wooden spoon, which is an unusual choice of verb. Sometimes you hear that a team 'claimed' the spoon, but even that suggests a certain deliberateness and desirability, like claiming your inheritance or your expenses from work. Perhaps one day we'll settle on an appropriate wooden spoon verb. 'Copping' the spoon could work. Being 'spanked' with the wooden spoon? Perhaps spoon itself will morph into a verb, like the nouns medal and podium have turned into the verbs 'to medal' and 'to podium' in the Olympics.

'So how'd the season go?'

'Bloody terrible, we totally spooned it.'

A spoontacular linguistic thing occurred only recently in Australian sport, when the Parramatta Eels and Wests Tigers played off for the wooden spoon (or rather, to avoid it) in the final round of the 2024 NRL regular season. Both teams were on the bottom of the ladder with just six wins, and happened to be facing off in Round 27, with the loser guaranteed the spoon. How did fans and media bill the match? In the tradition of America's Super Bowl, they called it the Spoon Bowl! Thus did two everyday kitchen items come to symbolise an epic battle for either humiliation or relief.

It was, of course, the Tigers who were humiliated 60–26 at home, thereby being paddled on the backside with their third consecutive NRL wooden spoon.

Great Aussie sporting terms: *Stone motherless last*

There is surely no richer source of uniquely Aussie sporting vernacular than horse racing. Some people think the sport is immoral.

Perhaps that's because they've never experienced the thrill of backing a moral. What does that even mean? In racing, a moral means a certainty or a sure thing, perhaps because it will secure a moral victory, as in a deserved win. Of course, any horse declared a moral is more likely to run stone motherless last. Stone motherless last???

As any racing person knows, it means a horse that can 'see the whole herd', as race callers also like to say. The origin of the phrase stone motherless last is unclear. Stone for stony broke, perhaps? Motherless as a reference to the old phrase that success has a thousand parents but failure is an orphan? Stone cold as in dead on arrival? There's a bar at Perth's Ascot racecourse with the amusing name of Stone Motherless, so maybe pop in there one day and ask. Just be sure not to pronounce 'Ascot' like the famous British racecourse, where the second syllable sounds like the latter half of 'biscuit'. Perth's racecourse is pronounced As-cot, like a sporting mascot, because the first rule of Australian sport is that it's not like British sport. Even though many of our most popular sporting pastimes originated in the UK, we play and talk about sport in a uniquely Australian way with shedloads of great Aussie lingo, and who cares if we sound like a bunch of drongos to the rest of the world?

ACKNOWLEDGEMENTS

Several high-profile sports media personalities and writers came off the bench to get around this project and their hard yards proved invaluable. They include Gerard Daffy, Rohan Connolly, Matt Cleary, Denis Carnahan, Glenn Cullen and many others. I'd also like to thank Nigel Wall for giving me a start on *Inside Sport* magazine way back in the early 2000s. Others in sports media whose support has proved invaluable along the way include Neil Breen, Heath Kelly and Alex Brown. Thanks to all at Hachette Australia and especially Sophie Hamley, a tennis tragic who is the Serena Williams of Australian book publishing. And of course, thank you to my family and to Pepper the naughty whippet for not eating the manuscript.

INDEX

Anthony Sharwood is a Walkley Award-winning journalist who has worked in TV, newspapers, magazines and online news. Formerly a sportswriter who covered several Olympic Games, he now specialises in the environment, climate and weather. In 2020 he released the acclaimed *From Snow to Ash*, a love letter to the Australian High Country written after walking the Australian Alps Walking Track, and in 2021 he explored the passionate environmental and cultural battle over Australia's wild horses in *The Brumby Wars*. His books *Kosciuszko* and *Bring Your A-Game* are both 2024 releases.

RUGBY
LEAGUE